UNDER A GIANT SKY

UNDER A GIANT SKY

SELECTED POEMS

TOON TELLEGEN

TRANSLATED FROM THE DUTCH BY
JUDITH WILKINSON

INTRODUCTION BY
ROBERT MINHINNICK

All rights reserved. No part of this work covered by the copyright herein may be reproduced or used in any means—graphic, electronic, or mechanical, including copying, recording, taping, or information storage and retrieval systems—without written permission of the publisher.

Printed by imprintdigital
Upton Pyne, Exeter
www.digital.imprint.co.uk

Typesetting and cover design by narrator
www.narrator.me.uk
info@narrator.me.uk
033 022 300 39

Published by Shoestring Press
19 Devonshire Avenue, Beeston, Nottingham, NG9 1BS
(0115) 925 1827
www.shoestringpress.co.uk

First published 2019
© Copyright: Toon Tellegen and Judith Wilkinson
© Introduction: Robert Minhinnick
© Cover image: Boris Tellegen
© Photo of author: Michael van Uden

The moral right of the author has been asserted.

ISBN 978-1-912524-44-0

This book was published with the support of the Dutch Foundation for Literature

**Nederlands letterenfonds
dutch foundation
for literature**

ACKNOWLEDGEMENTS

Translations included in this collection, or earlier versions of these translations, have appeared in the following journals, anthologies and art publications:

Acumen, *The Best of Poetry London 1988–2013* (Carcanet 2014), *De Hofjeskrant*, *Dutch*, *The Enchanting Verses Literary Review*, *Ina Brekelmans tekent de slatuinen* (art book, Blackbirdprint 2008), *The Manhattan Review*, *Modern Poetry in Translation* (2013 and 2019), *MPT Centres of Cataclysm* (Bloodaxe 2016), *A Poetic Celebration of the Hudson River* (Carcanet 2009), *Pushcart Prize Anthology 2013*, *Shearsman* and *Strike up the Band: Poems for John Lucas at 80* (Plas Gwyn Books 2017).

I am grateful to Toon Tellegen for his input, and for always being willing to discuss possibilities.

I would like to thank my mother, Han Wilkinson-Dekhuijzen, for her feedback and Anthony Runia for his extensive input.

I am greatly indebted to the Dutch Foundation for Literature for providing a translation grant.

Thanks are also due to Toon Tellegen's publisher, Em. Querido's Uitgeverij B.V., for permission to print these translations.

This publication has been made possible with financial support from the Dutch Foundation for Literature.

CONTENTS

Introduction 1
Translator's Preface 6

1980–1990

Flying Backwards 11
When Your Mother Dies 12
The Man 13
Ovid 14
Evening 15
Theseus 16
Ulysses 17
Charon 18
The Museum 19
With Impunity 20
Under a Giant Sky 21
The Other Knights 22
A Wadeable Place 23
A Summer House in Russia 24
A Letter 25
An Essay 26
Nocturne 27
We Travelled through the Night 28
A Melodrama 29
Peace 30
Under a Tree 31
A Fairy-tale 32
I Wrote to You 33
The Flower 34
A Conversation 35
A Very Bright House 36
Sometimes, in a Polder 37
There Are Hours 38
Desperate Door 39
And It Just so Happened 40
When I Wanted to Write to You 41
But He Forgot 42
A Man 43

1990–2000

Life and Myself	47
I Knew Someone	48
I Don't Want	49
A Miracle	50
An Apple in a Bowl	51
March 1300	52
The Muse	53
A Man Fell	54
September	55
The Discovery	56
A Boy	57
A Man Went for a Walk	58
A Man Walked and Became a Skeleton	59
I Was Allowed to Choose	60
Young	61
An Ambush	62
Once People Had Grown up	63
There Are Hundreds of Gods	64
I Was Skating	65
A Kiss	66
Never Happy	67
Ridiculous…	68
I Had to Say Something	69
A Man and His Thoughts	70
Occasionally	71
The Room of the Apples	72
One Morning	73
Only Just	74
Deep down	75
If It Was Night	76
A Man Fought with the Intolerable	77
A Man Tore Himself Apart	78
There Are Saints in the Streets	79
Just in Time	80
A Man Didn't Want to Make Anyone Sad	81
Everything Was Inescapable	82
Longing	83
The Question	84

A Line	85
Shall I	86
Facing the Truth	87
Sleeping Beauty	88
A Landscape	89
The Emperor Is Cold	90
Peace	91
On Dying	92
After Death	93
Leaving	94
Two	95
China Vases	96
At a Window	97
If There Were Two People	98
The Straight Road	99
Sunday	100
For a Long Time All Goes Well	101
Alone	102
You and Me	103
In the Inferno	104
A Mother	105
What I Expect from a Poem	106
With Your Ear to the Wall	107
Always Further	108
Freedom	109

2000–2010

If I Was a Flower	113
What You Must Do	114
The One Resigns Himself to the Facts	115
Don't Leave	116
The One Rests His Head in His Arms	117
I Say What's Possible, Says the One	118
The One Wants Peace	119
Quiet	120
The One Always Knows Better	121
The One Says Love Will Conquer	122
Going down	123
To Prevent Is Better	124

The Emperor	125
Something I Don't Know	127
What I'd like to Be	128
She Walks	129
At the End of the Day	130
At Night	131
The End Justifies	132
No One Can Serve Two Masters	133
One Swallow	134
From the Answer to the Corinthians	135
Long Ago	136
My Friend	137
What Two Women Saw	138
No	139
A Letter	140
You Should	141
A Moment	142
Two Women	143
A Man	144
My Father Applied a Double Standard	145
My Father Created the World	146
My Father Fished for Answers	147
My Father Slept through Headaches	148
My Father Was Gone	149
My Father Explained Himself	150
My Father Bowed to the Inevitable	151
My Father Was Already Himself	152
My Father Promised Everything	153
My Father Wanted to Love My Mother	154
My Father Got under the Skin	155
My Father Was so Small	156
My Father Was Coming to an End	157
My Father Began to Confuse Things	158
My Father Was Something	159
My Mother	160
Zeno	161
I Was Young	162
My Brother	163
Wings	164

Love and Death	165
Sorry	166
To Err	167
Distance	168
Daughter	169
Too Far into the Sea	170
A Poem for Henry Hudson	171
Sunset	175
It Was Raining	176
I've Come to Fight with You	177
A Man Thought That He Was Free	178
An Angel Looked at a Man	179
A Man Said: I Can't Live	180
A Warm Day	181
Evening	182
A Man Declared War on Himself	183
A Man Collected Questions	184
A Man Is Fighting with an Angel	185
In the End	186
Winter	187

2010—The Present

They Who Climb without Falling	191
Pain	192
The Writer Examines His Words	193
Alone with the Reader	194
Homecoming	195
Words He Can't Write	196
The Writer Cherishes	197
The Differences	198
In the Beginning	199
Trust	200
Reality	201
The Impossible	202
The Thought	203
I Wonder	204
A Garden	205
Weather Forecast	206
For an Old Friend	207

What to Say	208
A Stranger	209
Pontius Pilate	210
Portrait	211
Francis of Assisi	212
There's Something in the Air	213
Evening	214
The Rearguard	215
Hunger, Pain and Anger	216
Loving	217
The Face of the past	218
The Enemy	219
My Mother	220
She Who Shakes Her Head	221
The Face of Simplicity	222
They Overlook One	223
Who's There?	224
My Neighbour	225

Unpublished Poems

A Woman	229
On Death	230
A Cupboard	231
Happiness	232
On Despair	233
My Feelings	234
A Straw	235
The Precipice	236
Dutch Source Texts:	238
English Collections from Which Some of the Translations Were Taken:	239
About the Author	240
About the Translator	241

INTRODUCTION

Tellegen's 'unpublished poem' 'On Death' is an unashamedly humorous treatise on his attempt to avoid the big subject.

ON DEATH

I don't want to talk about death any more—
I start every encounter, every conversation by saying:
'let's not talk about death.'

if someone says:
'nice weather today'
I say:
'certainly not weather for discussing death'

I tell everyone that death is such a mundane,
*   not to say banal topic—*
you'd think there's nothing else to talk about:
love, for instance…
but no, death, death, always death…
I refuse to answer any more questions about it,
or fill in questionnaires,
or take part in conferences and chat shows on the subject

if someone asks:
'are you coming to the beach with us?'
I say:
'only if we don't mention death even once all day'

and then I go to the beach,
but alone—
the other person can't possibly live up to my demand—
I dig a hole in silence
from that hole I watch the surf, the sun, a freighter,
a yacht, gulls, children, kites, surfers,
dogs running about freely, dark clouds appearing on the horizon,
I toss back a ball that comes rolling my way,

I put a towel over my head,
rub sun lotion on my nose and cheeks
and with almost superhuman willpower,
filling me with immense pride,
I stop thinking about death.

Wry. But sly. Sometimes Toon Tellegen's wryness becomes surreal but this writer's tone is always intensely humane.

Because Tellegen is usually amused—sometimes hugely—by *life*, not death. What other possible response, he seems to enquire, might there be to the whole business? Thus for me Tellegen's poems are a series of intellectual shrugs. But Art as a coping mechanism? Indubitably. Surely that's one of its vital roles.

Tellegen is no nightingale yet his head is forever cocked. He is a bird sometimes irked but never vexed. I'd say Toon Tellegen is a fair mimic. Yes, he's a starling, of course. Starlings are quizzical creatures, clever and wonderful mimics. But they are also drawn to vast gatherings, and this poet could never be thought of as one amongst a flock, a single speck in one of those marvellous murmurations.

Neither is Tellegen a ventriloquist. Yet, he's sardonic, I suppose. Now, that's a certainty. Sardonicisms are a feature of his poetry but he is rarely, if ever, disdainful. No, Tellegen is too wise to belittle. Sarcastic, then? No, he's cleverer than that.

It does not require a detailed reading on my part to understand that Tellegen's subject is not God, existent or otherwise. Instead, the poet writes about *time*. Time is inescapable, running not only over, and around, but through us and our world.

Maybe it's been easier for this reader to come to terms with Tellegen when I consider what appears missing from his poetry. There is almost no 'description' in this work, little depiction of either urban or rural worlds, no elemental symbolism applied to other creatures. Of the natural world, indeed, there exists hardly a trace. 'Duckweed' (of all things!), mentioned below, comes as a surprise.

This is difficult for a 'British' reader, brought up on poetry that lauds 'creatures', and even celebrates the paltry, the literary, and maybe now the imaginary remnants of 'the wild'. What we have instead with Tellegen is intense self-examination. Thought linked, yes, with puzzlement, but rarely with bafflement. Tellegen is a writer imagining, listening to, and sometimes it appears, heeding, his own mind.

But what else is not present? There is little sonic playfulness in this poetry, also a dearth of what some might characterize as 'ornamentation'. For anyone conversant with the Celtic languages of Britain, this poetry might appear stark. Indeed, looked at this way, on the surface it seems to be curiously empty. Instead, with Tellegen, abstractions grind against each other like river icebergs in the Rhine. But they make a unique music.

Maybe the Dutch poet he most closely resembles is Judith Herzberg, another wry eye. Yet if Tellegen's poems are an assortment of shrugs, he is never indifferent. And hardly cynical. No, Tellegen cares, maybe too much. His poems inhabit a world of nuances, and his epiphanies miraculously exist without colour.

However, when we examine them, Tellegen's cataclysms comprise mundanities. His music exists without melody and yet it is instantly recognizable. Perhaps he is a laureate of the quotidian.

But where does any poetry begin? Surely with repetition (any parent would say), then in nursery rhymes. Having disposed of these ingredients (in his poetry at least, for he is also a successful children's writer), from here Tellegen creates poems when thinking about death, thinking about happiness, thinking about despair, and, above all, thinking about thinking itself. This writer makes his poems out of concern for philosophical conundrums. But such rhetoric is unanswerable.

Certainly, Tellegen is an ironist. Irony is fundamental to his poetry. And yet there is little obviously ironic in his poetry.

But yes, he is a satirist. In 'My Feelings' he mocks (surely?) our addiction to social media. Toon Tellegen is a satirist, then? Satire is maybe an underused weapon in current poetry's armoury, too subtle for Facebook and its newer rivals.

MY FEELINGS

I wish I could express my feelings

sometimes I hook them out at night:

Oh feelings,
dear little feelings,
why can I never find words for you,
you're so beautiful, so sweet...

then they bite me, jeer at me,
beautiful? sweet? we're not beautiful and sweet at all!
be glad!

my god, how they despise me...

then I fall asleep,
with lockjaw, a sardonic grin,
            the hullabaloo of a breath of wind.

Quite soon in any engagement with Tellegen, the reader will decide it's 'meaning' in life that the poet seeks. The title poem here is a good example:

UNDER A GIANT SKY

Under a giant sky—so grey and heavy
that I'm reminded of a Sunday
after a funfair in a city square—
I discover the thin thread between myself and...
but once again I don't know what it is
or who
and I step on a shell I hadn't seen
and I stumble.

I walk along a beach, through the roughest sand,
and above me hangs a balloon
in the lost sky
forever.

There is something, a person in my head says.
There should be something.

Maybe Tellegen's poems are his discoveries that there is no 'something'. Meaning is meaningless and art is a doomed search that discovers merely meaninglessness. And if there's 'nothing' now there never has been 'anything'. Yet the process of finding this out is... *fun*. Indeed, it is *life* itself. And of course, interrogating that 'person in my head' in the process creates the poems. Thus:

A WADEABLE PLACE

There is a wadeable place in me
But be careful, don't cause any ripples,
leave the rubbish alone in the duckweed
and let the fish sleep,
don't wave at anyone on the shore
and don't ask the sun for any shimmering
or the wind for any murmuring,
and feel how cold you are and how the water
is silver from a cupboard,
a candlestick
held against your cheek. Shiver, but invisibly,
and forget the other shore.
Wade, keep on wading, until you yourself
become wadeable
and no one will save me.

From that hole he has dug in silence Tellegen has learned that expectation is better than arrival. Maybe the gorgeous mundanity of his poetry is telling us it's time to grow up.

— Robert Minhinnick

TRANSLATOR'S PREFACE

In the Netherlands, where Tellegen is practically a household name, there have already been several anthologies of his work published, the most recent one, *Een van ons zal omkijken* ('One of us will look back'), compiled by Tellegen this year for his publisher, Querido. With more than a thousand poems to choose from by now, it seemed the time was ripe for an English selection of his work. I consulted Tellegen, and he made a selection of his own favourites, one hundred poems in all, taken from the long list of collections that have appeared over the years. He kindly allowed me to add all my own favourites, and the selection ended up being about half mine, half his.

Tellegen is a poet of endless surprises; as George Messo comments, in his review of Tellegen's *Raptors*: 'just when you think you've got the measure of the poem, Tellegen somersaults over your hand and off the page.' And yet he is also in many ways a very consistent poet, in that his work is always unmistakably recognisable as his. Although the work chosen here represents different phases of his writing, I hope the flavour, the momentum, the tone and the absurdist perspective weave together this motley collection.

I also hope the selection reflects the range of Tellegen's work: there are the wittily philosophical poems and the less dialectical, more whimsical poems—though the whimsy is never gratuitous. As an author who knows his classics, Tellegen has also written many poems that contain mythical elements, such as 'Theseus' and 'Ulysses', or are inspired by his beloved Dante, such as 'March 1300' or 'In the Inferno'. In making my own selection, I decided to include poems that are like forerunners of later work, such as the poem 'Mother', in which the mother figure, who 'wanted to walk very softly', is reminiscent of the often helpless mother in Tellegen's celebrated collection *Raptors* (Carcanet, 2011). I also included work on recurrent themes, such as Tellegen's ruminations on death and the poems preoccupied with fairy-tales, such as those that dwell on 'The Emperor's New Clothes' and 'Sleeping Beauty'. In addition, I chose numerous more lyrical poems, for instance the strangely haunting 'With

Impunity'; love poems like 'Peace' and 'You and Me'; and the moving poem 'Daughter'.

All Tellegen's collections published in the Netherlands are represented in this compilation, except for *De Optocht* ('The Procession', Querido, 2012), a tightly-knit sequence that was too long to be included in full. This book also contains about fifty poems taken from three earlier collections published in the UK: *About Love and About Nothing Else* (Shoestring, 2008), *Raptors* (Carcanet, 2011) and *A Man and an Angel* (Shoestring, 2013). In addition, one long, commissioned piece, 'A Poem for Henry Hudson', has been included in full here, which was first published in *A Poetic Celebration of the Hudson River* (Carcanet, 2009).

Dividing the book into chapters based on all Tellegen's publications in the Netherlands would have made it too fragmented, so I decided to divide it into decades, ending with some unpublished poems that Tellegen asked me to incorporate.

Translating Tellegen's poetry is always a delight. I am grateful for his quick feedback and the freedom he gave me. I tried to capture the originality of the source texts, aiming at the same concentration and liveliness. Tellegen told me once, when I was working on *Raptors*, that he attempted to use important words as few times as possible, and he encouraged me to find as many synonyms as I could for words (e.g. 'caressed', 'stroked'). I have done the same in this book, and I tried to find the kind of words that fit Tellegen's 'universe'.

I hope this book offers new surprises for Tellegen lovers and will entice those who are unfamiliar with his work to explore all the poetry—as well as the prose—that has already appeared in an English translation.

– Judith Wilkinson

1980–1990

FLYING BACKWARDS

I dreamt a poem about flying backwards:
I flew backwards and someone said
(she who, in my dreams, won't tell me her name):
that's impossible, an aeroplane doesn't fly backwards.
I said: I'm not an aeroplane.
No, she said, with strange anger, it is forever impossible.
And I went on flying, backwards,
with broad, long strokes.

WHEN YOUR MOTHER DIES

When your mother dies,
the door of a wild garden
closes,

a garden everyone had forgotten

When you yourself die,
who knows,
you might crawl back up
through the earth
into that old garden
where your mother is sleeping
in a wicker rocking chair
while caterpillars emerge
in the winter sun
and you can begin
your first dream again.

At your mother's feet
you no longer think
of death.

THE MAN

How elegantly he dives off a board into the wintry pool.
The mosaic in the concrete has faded
and is covered in snow here and there.
In one wonderful blink of an eye he takes it all in,

but time has stopped for him, for him alone.
He's been suspended in mid-air for years,
stretched out, heading straight down.

OVID

When dawn arrives with mist and the sounds of shouting
and the dogs of sleep have slunk off hungrily,
then he writes—
with his curious, sweet pen—
a letter to his enemy, the most august one.
He writes:
'There is no room in me for still more wounds.'

On his roof he hears the patter
of a barbaric sparrow.

EVENING

I'm on a train headed for a summer house in the north
and the scent of wood blows through the open window
of my room on a canal.
Evening.
Beside me sits my grandfather, blind and devout,
wearing a long black coat.
He sighs.
And that woman over there, with the serious expression,
spilling her tea,
that's my mother: I hadn't expected you,
she says, so far from home.
She pushes my books out of my hands,
making them tumble onto the floor,
and takes me with her in her thoughts:
the sun is shining, it's Sunday, everyone is out for a walk,
greeting people they don't know,
everyone is reading Gogol in the fresh grass,
everyone is wearing white clothes, everyone
bends over a picnic basket,
and suddenly she's gone, and someone
puts on his boots.
My grandfather and I, we're both sighing,
but only he is praying
as we continue our journey northwards. Someone
puts a key in the lock.

THESEUS

I knew I'd never see him again.
This had been predicted, I don't know
by whom.
He would throw himself off the cliffs when he
saw my ship return.
I thought: why, why at that moment? Jealousy? Madness?
Impossible!
But I knew how sly the Fates are.
Perhaps he'd leap high into the air,
climb onto wobbly stones,
sing a reckless hymn on a protruding rock,
grow dizzy with pride:
I, his son, saviour of the world and of his city…
Perhaps joy made him fall,
the joy of seeing my ship again.
I was slyer than the Fates
who cut all threads,
I hoisted black sails and slowly headed for the coast.

ULYSSES

I'm a shipwrecked person
and this is the sea
that I fear.
The giant eye above me is moved
to tears
about the nature of life.
All I'm bothered about are my companions and a beach,
and later perhaps a woman too, I'm not sure,
and a son.
And slowly the sea is evaporating
and I become a hero
and then a figment of the imagination.
I am the object of a strange suspicion,
unless I make a decision now
and drown unexpectedly.

CHARON

In his freshly tarred house full of young cobwebs,
on the banks of his green river,
while swallows skimmed past the last willows
and loose coins shimmered in the grass,
he lay sleeping.
His boat had sprung a leak or it was too late
or the wind was too strong or he was tired.
I wasn't planning to embark myself,
but I wanted to know who he was,
as a precaution,
and perhaps hear the lapping of the waves
and the sighs coming from the other side.
It was the middle of a day and when he woke up
and saw me standing at his window,
he immediately began to comment on my nails,
which he couldn't see,
and my croaky voice,
which he couldn't hear,
and my thoughts,
which he couldn't read, or perhaps he could,
and my shabby raincoat. What about yours, I replied,
pointing at all its holes.
I walked away, without knowing where to, while he called after me.
And when I looked back, tired of being so hesitant,
he was taking someone else with him. She was standing upright,
alone, in the middle of his boat.
She was wearing a green rose between her green-painted lips
and waved
from the middle of the river,
or was she coming towards me?
I saw wisps of smoke, reed and blurry figures
and a glistening other shore
and I no longer knew
if I was still there
or here already.

THE MUSEUM

In the Museum of Domestic Bliss
I saw the famous shards.
But when I enquired after the Mother,
the attendant gave me a grave look.
She's temporarily on loan elsewhere, he said.
I came to the room
of the Same Old Dreams.
I breathed in the aroma of a forgotten soup
in a display case at a window,
and on a wicker sofa sat the visitors
who'd just dropped in.

I headed home, bought some flowers on my way,
for in a vase.

WITH IMPUNITY

I will forget you and meet you again.
I will forget you, meet you and forget you again.
I will meet you again.

I will forget you and forget you and forget you again,
I will walk through dozens of parks,
pale green, violet and pink parks, inconspicuously,
in the rain.

In the evening I will forget you again.

The steps of the staircase won't remember
your name.
But they'll creak.
The front door will hesitate again.

UNDER A GIANT SKY

Under a giant sky—so grey and heavy
that I'm reminded of a Sunday
after a funfair in a city square—
I discover the thin thread between myself and…
but once again I don't know what it is
or who
and I step on a shell I hadn't seen
and I stumble.

I walk along a beach, through the roughest sand,
and above me hangs a balloon
in the lost sky
forever.

There is something, a person in my head says.
There should be something.

THE OTHER KNIGHTS

The one knight is insignificant,
the damsel is worm-eaten
and musty,

but the other knights!
They're still on their quests, riding crisscross through the land.
They're still following the swans to the south
and the wildest rumours to the north,
into a valley cut short by a mountain.
They're still confronting travellers, discovering swamps
and new tributaries.
They're still teetering, tumbling, exhausting themselves
and letting their nerves get racked.
They still dare to sell their souls,
they know what it means to be lost, they know the true nature
of doubt.

Oh, the other knights!
They set off in the same high spirits.
They will never wake up.

A WADEABLE PLACE

There is a wadeable place in me.
But be careful, don't cause any ripples,
leave the rubbish alone in the duckweed
and let the fish sleep,
don't wave at anyone on the shore
and don't ask the sun for any shimmering
or the wind for any murmuring,
and feel how cold you are and how the water
is silver from a cupboard,
a candlestick
held against your cheek. Shiver, but invisibly,
and forget the other shore.
Wade, keep on wading, until you yourself
become wadeable
and no one will save me.

A SUMMER HOUSE IN RUSSIA

A distant relative

Time stood still and the clock stood still,
the singing of the blackbird in the garden stood still
and the cat stood still, the cat stood still, stalking.
The passing car in the park stood still,
the poplars stood still
and the wind stood still, it suddenly stood still
in the middle of a gust of wind,
and even autumn stood still, just before winter,
autumn stood dead still, in all its bleak brilliance,
while an old man was trudging along a sandy road,
on and on,
in the north near a white sea,
and in the south
en route to Samarkand.

A LETTER

I forgot something,
I don't think you know this or believe it,
but when you visit me,
let's say I'm a house,
I live somewhere at the back,
I don't even know exactly where,
the lights never work,
you need to go up a few staircases, turn a few corners
and then go down a few steps.
The window looks out on an inner courtyard
where my mother is usually busying herself
with something or other,
and if she isn't there, she's about to arrive,
and she'll tap on the window modestly.
The bed creaks impressively
and keeps the neighbours awake .
Even on those rare occasions when you
manage to find me,
even then I probably won't be at home,
and you'll have to wait and see
if I haven't left for good this time,
something that happened only recently.
If nevertheless you still want to be with me,
which I can't imagine,
and I am at home,
then I'll be in that room in a corner under the table
with the low-hanging tablecloth,
where you'll never be able to find me
if you don't read this.

AN ESSAY

If you were to ask me: how old would you like to be,
I would say: 2420 years.
For then, as a boy in Athens,
I would have seen
Aristophanes' plays,
I would have borrowed the poems of Archilochus
from Euripides
and learnt them by heart,
and I would have heard what Socrates
said to his judges:
>   The hour of departure has arrived,
>   and we go our ways—
>   I to die and you to live.
>   Which is the better, only God knows.
Perhaps even back then I would have thought:
>   But I know too,
>   I know!

And in the spring I would have visited
the temple of Poseidon
and asked him
for distant journeys.

NOCTURNE

Some days are quieter and dustier
than ever

and only with the greatest effort
will some light fall on a tiny corner
of a windowsill
and a plant or a vase may appear there,
filled with hazy lilacs.

Perhaps a tiny long-suffering remnant of light will move
towards a table,
hesitate before a copybook,
perhaps a few words will jump up there, startled,
and see at last who is writing them.

But outside the sun still sets, as black as jet,
the stars still sparkle inkily,
every firefly still cloaks itself in smoke.

Occasionally a brief afterglow illuminates the darkest things,
dust, beetles, nooks and crannies.

WE TRAVELLED THROUGH THE NIGHT

We travelled through the night in a glossy black coach,
pretending we knew where we were going
and what the names were of the villages we passed,
pretending to know the coachman
and the night
and who we were
and why we kissed
and why we went off the road.
As we travelled through the night,
the night travelled through us,
scattering its commands over us
and into the depths
between us.

A MELODRAMA

In a park. A man.
He's angry because nobody is angry. Dogs
are snoozing in the grass,
and he's angry because somebody is angry. Seams tear
in somebody's new suit,
and he's angry because everybody is angry. The sun
gets up every nose on every bench, inserts itself into every newspaper,
and he's angry at the butterfly on the flower in the shrubbery
and at yesterday's caterpillar, and at the flower,
and at a pink skirt, a knee, a black shawl, a foot,
a small silk foot,
and he's angry about not being angrier,
or dead,
that's how angry he is.
Then he faints
and turns into a cloud
and then into a drop of rain,
and he wakes up pale with rage, seething,
and sighing deeply, one morning
on the banks of his soul.

PEACE

The peace between you and me
is a dragonfly. Wonderfully beautiful. Sparkling
in the evening sun, skimming
the foolhardy water
between you and me.

UNDER A TREE

Sitting under a tree, I met Death,
who explained something and then stopped talking and walked off.
I meant nothing to him, he said.
'But I am real,' I said.
'That means even less to me,' he told me.
'Is there anything that does mean something to you?' I cried.
'I don't think so,' he cried
over one of his unparalleled shoulders.
I started to feel cold, the sky was blue
and unrelenting.
Towards evening the wind rose, shrubs woke up
and the horizon turned red.
The whole place was still teeming with ants,
but the crows seemed pensive, barely cawing on the branches
of my tree.
After all, I was already lost.

A FAIRY-TALE

The emperor took off his coat
and all the people took off their coats.

The emperor hesitated
and all the people hesitated wholeheartedly.

The emperor put his coat back on
and they all hastily put their coats back on, fumbling,
wrestling with sleeves, stumbling.

The emperor was cold
and everyone shivered, stamped their feet, froze, fell
to their deaths

and a boy said,
a boy in a red coat holding his dead father's hand:
'You were going to show me the truth.
Where is the truth?'

I WROTE TO YOU

I wrote to you not to have any illusions…,
I told you that straightaway, the very first time,
I'd written it down in a note I carried with me
and I scrawled it on the edge of a newspaper
and on a calendar on your wall,
and I spoke it in your ear, in the doorway,
and in the street, on a quayside,
I called it out to you across the water,
in the light of a swaying street lamp,
and you called back:
I love you too!

THE FLOWER

What should I do with my summer, the flower wonders.
Blossom! And is that all? That's all!
And with my autumn? Wilt! And is that all? That's all!

An afternoon at a window, between two lace curtains.

And with my winter, the flower wonders,
what should I do with my winter?

A CONVERSATION

'Where shall we say goodbye?'
'In the rain.'
'Shall we take shelter?'
'No!'
'How will we feel?'
'Sick, mean and embarrassed.'
'What will we say?'
'We won't know.'
'What will we think?'
'If only it were yesterday, tomorrow or never.'
'Will one of us be in the right?'
'Neither of us will be in the right.'
'Will we each go in a different direction?'
'We will each go in a different direction.'
'Will we look back?'
'One of us will look back. Stand still, hesitate and look back.'

This is how they talked to each other, over and over again.
But they never asked who. Who
would look back. Who.

A VERY BRIGHT HOUSE

I live in a very bright house. I'm light-hearted
as I walk about, entering every room.
And if the curtains are shut, I open them,
see new curtains, curtains that ripple and rustle,
     taut curtains, fraying curtains with holes in them,
          grubby, dusty curtains, with velvet spiders.
The faintest scent of tea lingers in the air.
After every curtain my ease retreats
and the light recedes.
In the deepest darkness I open a window.
But I didn't know I could fly, all my wings
ache, the most terrible ache.

SOMETIMES, IN A POLDER

Sometimes, in a polder, between a few willows,
lime trees,
a train comes into being.
First a wheel, or first just something shiny
in the grass, a piece of rail
and then a wheel and then a carriage
and before you know it
the train drives off as cows
scatter,
it whistles and crunches,
the ground subsides, a gate
shatters
and where that train is headed and what
can still stop it, I don't know,
for I'm on board, I've paid my fare
and fall asleep in the darkest compartment.

THERE ARE HOURS

There are hours
without you. Occasionally. Perhaps. It's not unthinkable.
There are rivers with banks full of buttercups
without you. Boats with stuttering engines, upstream,
without you.
There are roads without you, side-roads, accidents,
ditches.

There are butterflies without you, thistles. Countless ones.
There is dejection without you. Indolence. Anxiety.
And not an hour passes,
not an hour has passed.

DESPERATE DOOR

Desperate door, in search of a house
with a bell, a corridor, a carpet and a lamp
(preferably copper, low-wattage),
as well as a threshold and a mat
and a half-hidden wooden staircase. Oh who
will let me swing open again in the night
when someone finally... or unexpectedly...?
Please write...

Whole cities wrote back, sent photos,
but the door couldn't make up its mind,
stood in the grass in the countryside far from any city
under a tall sky,
a red door.

There is a red door in the countryside
and still nobody enters anywhere,
and the wind keeps dragging muddled sentences
out of all the houses
that have no door.
There's draughtiness and sorrowing,
and tears well up in the sky.

AND IT JUST SO HAPPENED

And it just so happened, one morning,
one humdrum morning,
that I forgot to live happily ever after.

I thought: what is it I've forgotten?
I combed through everything I owned,
clutched at sneaking suspicions,
rejected improbabilities with some effort,
knitted brows, bit nails,
turned seconds over and over,
said: if need be… or: no matter what…
or: I will…
I was prepared to do absolutely anything,

but I didn't find what it was,
that one thing I'd somehow forgotten
one morning.

WHEN I WANTED TO WRITE TO YOU

When I wanted to write to you,
the word 'not' was missing.
Impossible, I thought, it's never
gone missing!
I pulled open all my drawers, searched everywhere,
before finding it
in the grass under two birch trees
among frayed cobwebs
in the sun, in a forest, unusable.

BUT HE FORGOT

But he forgot to kiss her
and when he left the castle it was quiet
behind him,
the air was grey,
the rose hedges tall and rigid,
a few sparrows scratched about,
but he was in a hurry, he didn't know why,
and when someone stopped him and asked
if it was dark already,
he didn't know that either
and said that it was probably still light
and that he was rarely wrong
and then he rode on.
When he got home everyone rushed at him: 'Well?
Did you kiss her?'
'Ah,' he said, 'that was what I forgot,'
and he kicked himself.
But when he returned at breakneck speed,
the castle had vanished, or perhaps it had never been there,
he didn't run into a single person and the scent of roses
was nowhere to be found.

A MAN

A man stopped everyone he came across:
'Are you Death? You?'
And one said:
'Yes, that's me' and another said:
'Who knows,' 'If only' or 'Now that you mention it...'
And that man walked away, he had big white feet,
he tripped over something bloody
and at that very moment, music began to play
and Death—huddled in a doorway,
hiding from life—cried:
'Hush... hush! Leave that dancing man alone!'

1990–2000

LIFE AND MYSELF

Life and myself—
a traveller stands still,
a country road in summer,
he's come from far.
Strange, he thinks, it's just as if...
and he slowly walks on again.

'Traveller!' I call out, crushed under his foot,
but moved, so moved...

I KNEW SOMEONE

I knew someone who,
when he was alone,
with no one on his mind, not even himself,
and certain that no one could see him
or hear him,
dug a hole in the ground
and spoke into it:
'I love you.'
Words that welled up in him from nowhere.

Reeds grew from that ground
and began to whisper, more and more loudly and melodiously:
'I love you. I love you.'
When a wagon drove past
one morning,
the wagoner heard those words
and let go of the reins.
The horses broke into a gallop, stormed up the slanting path
to heaven—
where there was nobody.

I DON'T WANT

'I don't want there to be anything eternal,
a paradise, celestial fields…!'
And somebody says:
'You're seeing it the wrong way!'
It's raining, it's bucketing down, and I reply loudly:
'Of course I'm seeing it the wrong way, I want to see it the
wrong way,
I want to see everything the wrong way,
everything!'
And there comes the tram, there is the famous crowd of people,
grey and in a hurry,
there is the night.

A MIRACLE

The painful thing about a miracle is
that you can't be surprised by it,
however much you want to,
it's impossible.

The painful thing about dying is
that you must always be surprised by it,
even though you don't want to and can't,
you must!

Why am I shouting?
I can hear myself all right.

AN APPLE IN A BOWL

There's an apple in a bowl
in front of an open window—
if it could think, the apple would think:
is this what overripe means, such a numb feeling…
The apple's still sweet,
but it's already growing tired, the way only an apple
can grow tired,
it's becoming wrinkled and discoloured.
It's a warm day, nothing quickens,
nothing happens
and a hand picks up the apple, turns it round
and throws it out of the window—
if it were able to be surprised, that apple
would be surprised and think:
is this what it means to be at your wits' end,
or is this bewilderment?
Evening comes, worms approach,
and the apple would think:
if I could still shine, how brightly I would shine…
That would be
its last thought.

MARCH 1300

The fires had gone out and all the ice was now water.
The devils gawped, scratching their backs with their forks.
Paolo and Francesca were squatting on the ground,
staring listlessly at their toes and occasionally
yawning at each other.
Geryon was asleep, Minos was asleep and Antaeus and Cacus
    were asleep,
as was Phlegyas, in his boat.
Cerberus was snoring softly, dreaming of enormous fields and
    beaches
and a friendly master.
The Erinyes kept their eyes closed and thought of nothing.
Even Lucifer was dozing, with his mouth open,
his jaws and thoughts at a standstill.
Only Ulysses was awake and still brooding:
if only I had ploughed on when…
if I hadn't persuaded Philoctetes…
if I'd let Ajax have those weapons…
if I'd stayed with Circe…
or with Calypso…
and hadn't shouted out that I was nobody…
if I'd never listened to Athena…
and if I'd gone on another voyage, with a small company—
we would have turned our oars into wings—
if only I had done *that*…
He would still have died peacefully, years later,
on Ithaca.
The air was stale and muggy—there was silence
in all the circles.
March 1300.
The wait was on for Dante.

THE MUSE

If you can lean out of a window,
then stretch to the point where you will either fall
or just, but only just, kiss her—

she will wait, her heart will pound, she will see
what your reach is.

A MAN FELL

A man fell,
dragging shrubs, blackbirds, beauty
down with him.
'Do that again,' a woman said,
and he fell again,
dragging melancholy and music and love
down with him,
and cupboards full of children.
'And again,' she said,
and he fell with a cry of pain,
dragging the sun down with him.
'And again,' she said,
and it grew cold around him—
he shattered into a thousand pieces.
'And once more,' the woman said,
and he fell again.

SEPTEMBER

September
and I picked a rose
and someone cried:
'That's not allowed! Those don't belong to you…'

The garden was empty
and everything around me was big and awe-inspiring:
the air, the grass, the trembling of my hand,
the rose that fell
and that voice, crying:
'Sorrow, *that* belongs to everyone…'

THE DISCOVERY

A man discovered the meaning of life,
ran outside,
stopped every passer-by, saying: 'Listen!
It's not at all what you think!'
and stumbling over his words
he explained it
to everybody
and everybody was astounded—
so *that's* the meaning of life…
ah, who would have thought it…
They shook their heads,
beat off flames,
jumped into ditches, rivers, cried for help,
walked away, lost in thought.

A BOY

I wish I was a boy, in 1860,
somewhere on the steppe,
a boy on a journey with his father,
who reads Lermontov to him in the evening—
hush!
in the middle of a poem—listen! krek! krek!
the corn crake—
a boy who lies awake at night,
his eyes shining,
outside, beneath the stars,
somewhere on the steppe,
and wishes he was a Phoenician
or a satrap of Alexander the Great.

A MAN WENT FOR A WALK

A man went for a walk and a woman flew past him through the air.
'That doesn't mean a thing to me!' he cried
and walked on.
A fine day, he thought. And that ocean of flowers!
Buttercups, dandelions, poppies, daisies...
And again that woman flew past.
His jacket began to crease.
His hair became tousled.
This is too much, he thought. Why can she fly,
while no one else can?
What could be behind this?
Some obscure logic?
Then she flew past again
and he fell on the ground.
I'm injured, he thought. How strange!
In the distance the sea murmured,
the sun went down,
cows were getting milked near a well under a poplar beside a ditch,
the air was red,
there were swallows, a scent of hay filled the air,
the moon came up.

A MAN WALKED AND BECAME A SKELETON

A man walked and became a skeleton,
lost his bones along a road,
one by one,
left and right,
until nothing but his pelvis remained,
one little wrist-bone
and his longing, ossified into a vertebra—

and a woman met him halfway, stopped him
and got to know him,
that longing,
that little wrist-bone
and that pelvis,
and she walked up hill and down dale
with that man—
until the past closed itself behind them.

I WAS ALLOWED TO CHOOSE

I was allowed to choose.
I didn't know what to choose.
I chose peace.

As for truth and beauty,
I let them go,
along with wisdom and wistfulness—
and even love
that gazed at me with such wonder,
while black clouds drifted in her wake.

Peace, there was peace.
And in the furthest outposts of my soul
creatures danced
that I'd never even heard of!

And in the sky hung a different sun.

YOUNG

I'm young,
I'm very young,
I'm extravagantly young, insanely young—
let's cry shame on me,
let's pitch bricks through my windows,
let's ignore me, turn our backs on me
and forget me—

and if we just happen to look over our shoulders,
to see if the sun is already setting and
the motionless herons are still perched beside the ditches,
then I hope I will have vanished,
with my flushed cheeks,
my wild oohs and aahs,
my blazing thoughts.

Later, much later, I may come back.
But reluctantly.
And old.

AN AMBUSH

A man hated himself with a smouldering passion
and frequently laid an ambush for himself
in order to settle the score
for good—
and he would prick up his ears,
feel his heart pounding,
wait for hours, days, lying stock-still in the shrubbery—

but he always took a different route.

ONCE PEOPLE HAD GROWN UP

Once people had grown up and become almighty,
which took a long time,
they found God,
somewhere shivering in the dark on the ground.
Well, well, God, they said, fancy meeting you here...
They shook their heads.
But not long after, they scattered bread,
put out small bowls of wine for him
and saw
how he hesitantly
came closer,
and very carefully, with one finger, they touched him.

THERE ARE HUNDREDS OF GODS

There are hundreds of gods—friendly gods, dejected gods,
wanton gods, small-minded gods—
and there is one human being
who, with eyes shut tight,
his fingers in his ears,
his head bowed,
perches on the edge of his chair
and stubbornly screams:
'I am the light! I am the darkness!'

I WAS SKATING

I was skating
and high up in the sky my mother flew along with me,
painting the sky purple for me,
putting the wind in a box
and preparing severe frost
for later that evening—
my father was smoking his finest cigars,
leaning on the horizon,
and in the reed I saw my children,
whose white, powdery plumes
rustled—
I skated and skated
and my mother cried:
'Shall I stop time, right now,
shall I do that?'
'Yes, all right,' I cried
and slowly skated out of her sight
into the grey distance.

A KISS

'Shall I give you a killer kiss?'
She stood on her toes, put her hand in my neck
and gave me a killer kiss,
one of those kisses that hangs by a silken thread
and swishes back and forth, spins on its axis and shoots away—

I couldn't stop it, I cried out, waving my arms about
and running after it—

one of those kisses that turns round
and takes aim, a bit higher, a bit lower,
one of those lethal kisses.

NEVER HAPPY

Some people can never become happy.
'Impossible,' they say.
And yet they suddenly become happy nevertheless,
jump up, run around,
try to shake off this happiness, roll through the grass,
leap into ditches, seas—

only one or two people pull themselves ashore again,
half dead, half alive,
drag themselves towards shrubbery,
hide and think:
now I will really never, never again be...
shake their fists at happiness—

towards evening it seizes them, overpowers them.

RIDICULOUS…

A man wanted to talk about love.
'No…! Not about love…!' everyone cried
and everyone left or knocked him down,
and death peered through a window:
'About love…? Ridiculous…!'

That man put on a pair of wings
like those of a thrush,
but larger and more despairing,
and away he flew and sang about love
and love sang about him, murmured about him—

never did a man go to bed more sorrowful
on the indifferent earth.

I HAD TO SAY SOMETHING

I had to say something.
I looked around me. Who were present?
I saw escapism, with his restless eyes,
and doubt, in his long, grey coat.
I saw ambition, in full regalia but crippled,
and dissatisfaction with the here and now.
Relativity was present too, hunched over
on a small stool in a corner—how could he not be present—
and responsibility with his enormous eyebrows—
      there's not much more to him than those eyebrows.
I saw the despair sisters, tottering on their white high heels,
forever ransacking their handbags
and casting each other questioning looks.
I also saw indifference and complaisance, with their backs
to me, and vanity, suspicion, hubris,
presumption…
But where was shame, my shame?
I looked aside, up, down,
and suddenly I saw her, out of breath, flushed and stammering:
'Am I too late?'

'I…' I said.

A MAN AND HIS THOUGHTS

A man, pounding his thoughts:
'You always, always make me sad!'
he flew at them,

and they shrank from him, pulled up their collars,
hunched their backs.
What should they do?

And that man walked along a road
and comforted his thoughts, apologised to his thoughts,
felt shame towards his thoughts,
promised them everything, everything,

in the light of the setting sun.

OCCASIONALLY

Occasionally,
with great effort and mainly by chance,
someone manages to
wrap both arms round his grief.
He lifts it up.
May the door not be locked, now...
He pushes it open with his knee
and walks outside, with big, broad strides.
Watch out! he cries,
for his grief is so big that he can't see beyond it,
and it's never transparent.
Far away, in a ditch or in some boggy spot
beneath poplars
or behind a crooked fence among old car tyres,
toys and the remains of a fire,
he throws it down

and walks home, whistling.

THE ROOM OF THE APPLES

In the room of the apples, the shy apples,
the red and the yellow apples,
in a white and crumpled bed:
my mother,
reading Anna Karenina, while eating an apple,
and deep in thought
she disappeared through a wall,
soundlessly she disappeared through a white wall that led
to apple orchards,
to apple pickers and apple gatherers and apple baskets and
    apple carts,
to apple barges with apple holds,
to apple ports and apple markets with apple sellers and
    apple boys,
to apple attics with apple spiders and secret
    apple crates and clouds of apple dust,
to warm apple nights
and ink-black apple skies, furious apple storms
and long apple winters in the heavy snow, the heavy heavy snow.

ONE MORNING

I remember it clearly:
one morning I woke up and knew that I was a Dutchman,
never anything other than that.
I was perhaps twenty
and felt like Gregor Samsa—too late,
above all too late.

How I've been since then:
I don't know,
I don't want to know.

But once in a while, at odd moments, I muster all my courage
and dare to dream that I'm not a Dutchman,
anything but a Dutchman.
Then I walk through the golden throne-room of my dream
slowly and wistfully, but with a light step—
until someone throws me an apple.

Look, it's me who's throwing it! Old Samsa!

ONLY JUST

I live happily ever after, but only just,
and there are people who only just love each other forever—

under a tree stands Newton,
gazing at an apple
that only just doesn't fall—
it's evening, it's raining, bedraggled herons are standing stock-still
at the side of a ditch,
while he gazes up passionately—

everything that is impossible is still just possible,
peace only just floats across the infinite countryside.

DEEP DOWN

Deep down I am a person
who sits in the grass
tossing pebbles into a ditch
while thinking:
I've had enough.

But deep down:
why would I want to go deep down...
I have no business there!
Just let me toss those pebbles
into that green ditch
with its morbid waterlilies and its immortal reed tufts—
I'm somewhere else,
at the edge of my thoughts—
I waver
and always want more.

IF IT WAS NIGHT

If it was night
and a door opened
and there were footsteps, nothing more than footsteps,

and we glowed, burned, were flames, lighting up the world
and the darkness around us—

would someone stamp us out then,
ingloriously and punctually,
and would those footsteps die away again then, in the distance
beyond the open door,

or would our flames blaze up higher and higher,
until Time discovered us—night watchman of our longing
and of all that was never possible?

A MAN FOUGHT WITH THE INTOLERABLE

A man fought with the intolerable,
a snail,
a worm in the mud of his soul.
'Why don't you shout something at me?' that man cried.
Silence.
The wind rose,
blew through the farthest corners of his soul,
blew against garden sheds,
kennels,
abandoned in the valleys at the edge of his soul,
lifted that man up,
swept him forward, raging, while he fought with the intolerable,
tumbling, glowing
in the morning light—
and a woman stood in the doorway,
on the threshold,
leaned against the door,
slowly opened his door.

A MAN TORE HIMSELF APART

A man tore himself apart and tore himself apart again
and again,
and after scrupulously examining what was left of him,
he tore himself apart again—
philosophers darted back and forth, like lizards,
scrambling to find their thoughts.
His lucid nature, his irresoluteness, his grubby shame:
everything was scattered far and wide.
Perhaps someone found him there
and brushed him clean, with the patience of a saint,
blew the dust off him,
put him back together again,
wiped her hands on an apron and lifted him up
and carried him away.
But perhaps, and it's not unthinkable, no one found him there
and he went on tearing himself apart over and over again—
until he was too small for his fingers.

THERE ARE SAINTS IN THE STREETS

There are saints walking through the streets.
You can recognise them by their inconspicuousness,
by their invisible cloaks,
    precious beyond measure,
billowing loosely round them,
and by their sorrow.

When we spot them, we walk past them.
But we hear a rustling sound.
When we look round, we see them separate themselves
    from other people,
quicken their pace and turn into side streets.
Everywhere people stop and look round.

It's time for us to turn into a side street,
but we're afraid to,

we'll end up in a worse plight then,
we'll lose our way then

and we'll come face to face then, in the rain,
in the night.

JUST IN TIME

Just in time they managed to What
did they manage just in time? For whom?
They managed to just in time Just in time
all wars ended,
silence returned,
life became musty and mulish again.
Just in time people have Just in time they've
started to daydream,
yawn,
just in time they're dying a colourless death again,
    instead of a magnificent, exuberant one.
A door opens,
 children are customers, eager, impatient,
 and the world, in its dustcoat, steps out of its twilight,
 and asks, with honeyed tongue:
'How can I help you?'
They don't know the word,
 they point at peace.

A MAN DIDN'T WANT TO MAKE ANYONE SAD

A man didn't want to make anyone sad
in any way, ever!
He rushed around, accosting everyone:
'Do I make you sad,
and you?'
Under plane-trees, in long lanes, in dark alleyways,
in the drizzly rain.

Evening came.
'And you?
And you?'

He collapsed,
cried one last time 'And you?' and fell silent,
and from his head rose enchantment, crimson and
    ultramarine…
'No! You don't make us sad!'
Blue lackeys in golden liveries carried him off, chanting,
lashed their whips at sadness

and a woman wept.

EVERYTHING WAS INESCAPABLE

Jealousy was young,
still dewy,
and love shuffled past the first corn ill at ease,
pricked itself on the first thorns,
didn't know what fright was yet
and bleeding.

In the distance lay the word: large, wrinkly and empty.

The laws of nature creaked, crunched,
got into their stride one by one.
Apples fell, leaves, stars.
Rivers flowed from the first mountains.

Cain raised his arm.
Everything was starting, everything was new,
everything was inescapable.

LONGING

Longing,
with countless fingers on its hand, fumbling,
floundering,
hears voices behind a hedge:
'Have you seen peace by any chance?'
'No.'
'Or happiness?'

It sees demons all around,
its own demons,
with their big, heartless eyes,
reclining lazily or climbing the air with a yawn
and attacking without qualms.

Longing cultivates roses and frenzied dogs,
rows across lakes as the sun sets,
shrieks.

THE QUESTION

'Does anyone know what love is?'
Every hand goes up.
'Who doesn't know?'

Only happy people don't know,
and only when they are exceptionally happy,
when they are wallowing and drowning in happiness, in summer,
in the glow of the setting sun.

'And does anyone know what leaving is?'
No hands go up.
'And staying?'

A LINE

I drew a line:
this far, and no further,
I'll never go further than this.

When I went further,
I drew a new line,
and then another line.

The sun was shining
and everywhere I saw people,
hurried and serious,
and everyone was drawing a line,
everyone went further.

SHALL I

Shall I leave?
Shall I grow sad and leave?
Shall I finally conclude life is insignificant, shrug my shoulders
and leave?
Shall I set the world down (or hand it to someone else),
thinking: this is enough,
and leave?
Shall I look for a door,
and if there is no door: shall I make a door, open it carefully
and leave—with small meek steps?
Or shall I stay?

Shall I stay?

FACING THE TRUTH

You must, they said, face the truth.
Now! Immediately!
I faced the truth.

When it grew dark, they whispered:
now you may face something else—
if you like.

It was quiet
and I faced love
and thoughtlessness with its giant wings
and the simplicity of the moonlight on my wall.

Now the truth again, they said. Now!

SLEEPING BEAUTY

Sleeping Beauty was asleep.
Beside her lay a letter:
> 'Don't kiss me awake.
> Under no circumstances.
> Not even after a hundred years.'

What shall I do? the prince thought. Shall I leave?
Or shall I kiss her, thinking she doesn't mean it?
I'm so tired, so dead-tired...

Sleeping Beauty peeked through her eyelashes.
With the greatest effort she took slow,
regular breaths.
She saw the door close,
heard the steps on the staircase—
so tired, so dead-tired, his every step—

and her heart broke.

A LANDSCAPE

I'm a landscape,
let's make a landscape out of me,
let's drive up in a car and get out,
let's look at me through a fence.

One of us should say:
there might be a treasure in this landscape,
let's dig for it,
let's find gold.

We climb the fence.
We dig.
We dig ferociously.
We find gold.
Gold! Gold!
But what do we care about gold, really?

We lean on our shovels.
High above us the clouds.
Let's be content with nothing,
let's drive on again.
The sun is allowed to set in this landscape,
is allowed to slide its last rays across the fields, across the tops
    of the trees, against the hillsides.
We drive somewhere else.
We sing, our windows are down, our radio is on.

THE EMPEROR IS COLD

The emperor is cold,
appears on the steps of his palace,
cries:
'Why don't I have any clothes on?'

Everyone keeps silent.
Men keep silent.
Women keep silent.
Those who know everything keep silent.
Children keep silent.

'Why?' cries the emperor. 'I must know!
Now!'

Soldiers take aim.
Searchlights sweep back and forth.
It's winter and I am a poet
who writes about love and about nothing, nothing else,
ever.

PEACE

Look, there goes peace.
Everyone jumps up.
Where? There! In that blue coat!
They press their noses against the window,
lean on each other's shoulders.
It's very small.
They've never seen it before.
They cry: peace! peace!
It doesn't hear them,
disappears from their view.

They feel their hearts pounding
and go back inside, grab hold of each other
and hesitate.
Should they kill each other or should they kiss each other?
What should they do?
Your call, they whisper.
No, yours.
No, yours!
Yours!!

ON DYING

Dying?? Never heard of it!

But one evening, under a streetlamp, I found a poem about dying.
It was rain-drenched and almost illegible,
but everything was in it.
I learnt it by heart and thought:
might there be just such a poem, such a rain-drenched, almost
    illegible poem,
about love, with everything in it about love,
and should I learn that by heart too?

AFTER DEATH

After death comes the hereafter:
nothing out of the ordinary,
except that everything is different.

Before death comes life,
but no one is sure of that.
Everyone has their eyes shut,
holds their breath:
it's coming, it's coming…!
Everyone thinks they can hear something already.

LEAVING

I will leave just once. Then I will stay.
Perhaps I will leave twice. But then I will surely stay…

After I have left, I will stop once
and hesitate,
perhaps twice—I don't know.

I am right, I'll think.
I will take the shortest road, the most beautiful road,
and the fastest road too,
the road past precipices and elegant ruins,
the road past poppies, past screeching gulls—

the road home.

TWO

Two people.
One is nice, the other is nicer.
One fishes up the truth,
   the other fishes up the truth and wrings it out.
One hides, the other hides and is unfindable.
One falls, the other falls and gets up again and falls again.
One clings to the other,
   the other clings to the one and scratches him, bites him,
   takes him by the throat, doesn't let him go.
One thinks of his beloved,
   the other thinks of his beloved and of the world
   and of the congruity of things and of St. Augustine
   and of fires blazing high.
One is alone,
   but as alone as the other
   only a dog can be, in a kennel, pining away.

CHINA VASES

China vases and china love
    with raspberry ice-cream and grenadine,
china hours
    with tea in china cups
and tiny china biscuits—

we receive a letter:
the meek send us their regards—

we are careful and common-sensical,
only on the inside do we shout for joy
and we reply cautiously:
'We eagerly await your china kiss…'

and yet,
and yet there's a bull—
smaller than a mouse, but nevertheless a bull—
a bull has woken in our soul,
in our slowly withering soul

and begins to stampede.

AT A WINDOW

I'm standing at a window.
I see words approaching.

Some words I recognise:
albeit, red, untoward,
notwithstanding—in a loose-fitting jacket—
forthrightness, slipshod…

Some climb onto each other's shoulders.
'Who are you?' they cry.
'Cloudy,' I cry.
'With bright patches or overcast?' they ask.
'With bright patches,' I answer.

I cast down my eyes.
I wish I were aflame
or appreciable
or, even better: nevertheless.

It starts raining.
Albeit looks up, her cheeks become moist.
Far and wide run away.

Darkness descends.

IF THERE WERE TWO PEOPLE

If there were two people
and the one loved me, indulged me,
never wanted to hear a word against me,
and the other mistrusted me,
was always on the lookout for me and my failings,
never let me be,
and I was allowed to forget one of them,
who would I forget?

And if they went to battle over me,
first with their fists and then with pointed weapons, firearms—
they're bound to hate each other—
who would win, I wonder?

And if I could intervene,
at the risk of my life:
would I intervene?

Meanwhile I keep dreaming of the Great Indisputability
with its whirling sands, its scudding clouds,
its bullfinches, its scent of resin...

THE STRAIGHT ROAD

I walked along a straight road
I called it a straight road
it wasn't a straight road

I reached a corner
I won't turn that corner, I thought
I turned that corner

I reached an even straighter road
I called it an even straighter road
just as I called what I was doing: walking
it wasn't walking

I reached another corner
I won't turn that corner, I thought,
I won't won't won't turn that corner
I turned that corner

I walked along a straight road
one morning I walked along a straight road
I called it a straight road

it was a straight road.

SUNDAY

It's Sunday,
the walkers are sitting on benches,
conversing about the sine and cosine of a kiss,
the tangent of desire.
They close their eyes and think about people they don't know,
x, y...

The sun is shining,
small hypotheses hum in the mellow afternoon light,
immaculate truth is asleep.

Everything is trifling and a fraction short of perfect,

and far away, infinitely far away, among wild ellipses
and red parabolas,
children are swimming
in a bend of a river.

FOR A LONG TIME ALL GOES WELL

For a long time all goes well,
rivers flow pleasantly to the sea,
flowers blossom,
butterflies dart about,
philosophers sleep in the broad shade of dualism,
people agree with each other,
life is gentle and generous,
girls whisper in ears:

> 'Let's... etcetera,
> Oh, let's always... etcetera...'

For a very long time all goes well,
for an improbably long time all goes improbably well.
All is still going well,

even now all is well
and now.

ALONE

I'm standing on a stage, alone.

I'm playing the role of someone who's about to enter,
who's standing in the wings,
who discards his lines, picks them up again and discards them again,
who hears whispers:
      'Speak clearly
      and in the direction of the audience…',
who clears his throat, feels his lips with his tongue
and thinks: why, why me…

someone who stretches and stretches the final second
with a force
      he hadn't suspected in himself…

Loudspeakers magnify the drumming of my heart.

The performance is nearly over,
for as long as I can remember.

YOU AND ME

'...and on that same day He created shame
and shyness,
but when evening came
and the lion was asleep beside the lambs,
He created something strange—perhaps He was tired,
perhaps He'd intended something else—
and He gave it a name: equilibrium...'

This is apocryphal,
but He didn't create anything stranger than this:
the equilibrium
between you and me.

IN THE INFERNO

During his descent in hell, Dante saw victors
wherever he looked:
popes, emperors, generals, philosophers.
But not a single loser.

I never looked into this, I never
read about this either—

but the smell of burning laurels,
the glow of melting signet rings,
the hollow truth...
and Charon, in his little house,
watching the new victors approach
on their golden, spindly legs...

Oh victors, in your turquoise coats,
you'll have to kiss your own hands now,
for you'll never have any more losers crawl for you—

the poplars rustle,
piglets root about at the water's edge.

A MOTHER

She wanted to walk softly.
She walked very softly.
But she thought she was stamping her feet.

Night set in, and she walked even more softly.
The wind rose and she thought she was stamping her feet very
    loudly now
and that everyone thought: who is stamping so loudly?
I, she thought. I am stamping so loudly.

She thought malice had stolen into her,
the way an adder sometimes steals into someone,
or a jackal,
or a spider.
She stood still, held her breath.
Now everyone is awake, she thought.
Now I have stamped everyone awake.

It was winter.
They searched for her, couldn't find her.
They called out for her to shout.
'We can't hear you!' they cried.

They were scared she would freeze to death.
They were at their wits' end.

WHAT I EXPECT FROM A POEM

I want to be able to step into a poem
as if it was a horse-drawn carriage.
I want to be able to say 'Giddy up' or 'All set!'

The sun must shine
and spectators must stop and call out to me:
'What's your destination?'

Mud must splash
and I must get shaken about like an elderly prelate,
while trying to steady myself
and replying:

'An unknown one!'

WITH YOUR EAR TO THE WALL

The wall mustn't be too thick
and not too thin either—
if the wall is too thick, you'll just hear murmurs,
if the wall is too thin, you'll hear everything.

You must catch a few words, fragments of sentences.
You must want to deny
or confirm something passionately.

Your ear must sting from the force
of pressing it against the wall.

You must feel your heart pounding
and know that now, really now...

You must control yourself.
You must always push yourself to the limit.

ALWAYS FURTHER

I always want to think further,
but I don't want facile thoughts,
I want obstacles to think my way around,
ambushes, crafty pitfalls,

and I don't want things to end well,
I don't want a lucky escape,

I want hostile thoughts
that force back my thoughts, injure them,
decimate them,

I want incinerated concepts and down-trodden ideas,
I want my thoughts to be forlorn,
while still feverishly making plans—
ill-fated plans, fabulous plans—

that's how I want to think,
for as long as I can think.

FREEDOM

For killing and being happy and holding back
and hesitating
and falling into an abyss
and denying and being guilty
and feverishly searching for truth, beauty—
freedom makes no difference,
or at most the difference between a flowering apple tree
and no flowering apple tree,
or between a kiss and no kiss, however fleeting
and treacherous it may be.

2000–2010

IF I WAS A FLOWER

If I was a flower,
would I blossom now?

Or would I be a special flower,
an unbelievable flower,
a flower that can't choose between blossoming
        and not blossoming

and leans over the edge
of a vase,
to see if his abyss has a bottom?

Or could I do nothing but blossom,
should I do nothing but blossom,
red and thoughtless,
on an unblemished mantelpiece, somewhere
between shame and joy?

And if I was a flower,
would I know when to wilt?
Not just yet?

WHAT YOU MUST DO

You must think hard.
You must use words that are all over the place.
Plumage. Ultramontane. Miserliness.
You must feverishly search for patience
and for simplicity and insecurity.
You must think up a decisive moment
that can approach at lightning speed
(faster than any other moment).
You must behave like an idiot.
You must dawdle.
You must be utterly unprepared for anything
and believe that you're nothing, not even futile, immaterial
or irrelevant,
and yet even then...

THE ONE RESIGNS HIMSELF TO THE FACTS

The one resigns himself to the facts,
calls out to the other: 'You should do the same!
They are so very soft and inaccurate…'

The other is going full tilt at the facts,
rips them apart, obscures them and throws them away.
'I am still fighting rearguard actions!' he exclaims
in a hoarse voice.

Outside dahlias and marigolds are flowering
and a yellow rose.

'I'm now dreaming,' the one calls out, 'the untidiest of
dreams…'
And I, the other thinks, am dying a rearguard death,
struck down by something gone astray.

DON'T LEAVE

Don't leave, says the one

and the other catches those words,
turns them over and over in his mind
and hurls them away
with the immense power of indecision.

Perhaps, he thinks, someone will find them—
someone who just happens to miss them—
somewhere
in some lost moment.

THE ONE RESTS HIS HEAD IN HIS ARMS

The one rests his head in his arms,
thinks of something new, something different,
something that doesn't start with a word
and with two people,
something without jealousy and dying,
and without bad taste, bad behaviour
      and irrepressible nonchalance,
but he can't think of anything
and falls asleep,

and next to him sits the other,
created in his image—
his face turned to the heavens,
timid, frightened and shy,

but he is awake
and thinks of everything,
everything he wants to think.

I SAY WHAT'S POSSIBLE, SAYS THE ONE

I say what's possible, says the one,
and I what's impossible, says the other.

They're sitting next to each other
in the charming desert of a room
full of luxurious music and pitch-black mirages—

who will be the first to speak the last word, the one wonders,
and who will slam the door shut behind him, the other wonders,
stop in his tracks,
turn around,
run back,
call out: I've forgotten something...

and who has not forgotten anything, the one wonders,
will never forget anything, ever.

THE ONE WANTS PEACE

The one wants peace,
kicks down doors,
breaks resistance,
demands tenderness,
burns things down,
shouts that timidity will save the world…

The other sharpens gentle knives.

'…or diffidence,' the one shouts, 'or the early morning light on the fields…'

The other whispers that he wants war.

QUIET

It's quiet—

the one stands at a window and looks outside,
the other stands at a window and looks inside,

the one fears a life of pain,
the other fears a life without pain,

the one is the enemy of the other,
the other is the friend of the one,

they approach each other,
armed to the teeth with incense, myrrh,

time presses, says the one,
stresses, says the other,

the curtains are closed, the table has been set,
the bed thrusts off its cover—

the silence before a slip,
before a rumour.

THE ONE ALWAYS KNOWS BETTER

The one always knows better than the other,
but the other

the one is also more sensitive than the other,
but the other

the one is so much bigger, so much more impressive than the other,
but the other

the one is human, nothing human is alien to the one,
but the other

the one points out ugliness and bitterness,
    warns against shame and jealousy,
        his arms filled with peonies and busy lizzies,
but the other

the one loves the other,
but the other

THE ONE SAYS LOVE WILL CONQUER

The one says love will conquer
and the other asks:
'On what grounds do you claim that?'
'Grounds? Claim?' says the one
and he waves injunctions and edicts about,
arrests the last defeatists
still sitting at the table
with giant plates of macaroni and bacon in front of them,
and hauls them away.

'...will conquer!'
His evil angels sing.

Who are you? the other thinks. Who are you
again and again?

GOING DOWN

Look, there we're going down…
they see themselves go down—

you almost imperceptibly, the one says
and you ardently and with style, the other says—

they show each other
the last rays of their restlessness,
the red glow of their desire—

they wait
until there's nothing left of themselves to see
or think,
they stand on tiptoe, waver for a moment,
and walk on,

in the resilient dusk.

TO PREVENT IS BETTER

God shakes his seriously doubted head—

if to prevent is better than to cure,
then he wouldn't have started anything,
then it would still be the hour zero
on day zero
and it would stay like that—

he bites his no longer imaginable nails
and peeks down—

soon he'll start curing,
and in his endearing wisdom he alone
knows the ailment.

THE EMPEROR

The emperor knew full well
that he wasn't wearing any clothes.
He himself had taken the weavers aside
and instructed them.

And when he appeared in the streets, we too saw only too clearly
that he wasn't wearing any clothes.
But when he shouted: 'I've got new clothes!'
we shouted: 'They're magnificent!'
and cheered.
Why should we displease him?
The truth is so mundane and so malicious.

Only that boy, holding his father's hand—
everyone said he was so bright...
and that he was bound to go far in life...
We chucked him into a ravine—
for the wolves to find.
'You don't have any teeth!' we cried after him.
'Why don't you shout that.'

Later he became an emperor himself,
as is fitting in a fairy-tale.
Not here, but somewhere far away.
From time to time we receive news from there:
he demands that his subjects say exactly what they think.
Those who keep secrets or make something up or bend the truth
or even sing something they don't mean
lose respect
or—if they prefer—the rest of their lives.

Our emperor is old now
and rarely appears in public.
When he does, he wears an old shirt
or a fraying pair of trousers.
People say he is senile.
But when we see him, we cheer
and cry: 'How young you look! How well everything suits you!'
Then he nods
and promises us wings that will allow us to fly
all the way up to the stars,
for truth is nothing.

SOMETHING I DON'T KNOW

I wish I didn't know what everyone knows.
What does everyone know?
That we all die in the end.
That's the only thing we all know for certain.
But I don't know that.
I'm the only person in the world who doesn't know that.

WHAT I'D LIKE TO BE

I wish I was a bit nicer, livelier, happier, faster, smarter, braver,
funnier, more exciting, more exceptional, more attractive
than I am now
and that someone would say to me:
'Oh no, you're perfect the way you are now.'

And I am! I know it!

SHE WALKS

She walks through my thoughts.
Up and down.
Sometimes she steps out, briefly,
then, in one great leap—glass shattering,
the frame breaking—she jumps back in.
Throbbing light
and throbbing memories—innumerable ones.
One will cause grief—in what dress,
with what scent?

And why does she never enter through the door,
why never shyly and uncertainly
just knock?

AT THE END OF THE DAY

At the end of the day,
when someone comes rushing in with love,
when you're tired and clumsy and just at that moment caught
in a tangle of fears—
what do you do,
what do you do with love, downy, easily frightened,
that someone still brings you?

AT NIGHT

At night, in the dark, under his horse blanket—
having seen his gruffness in mirrors—
Newton thinks:
'But does the apple *wish* to fall,
does God *wish* to exist…'

and see, the wish walks across the waters,
and on his shoulder gravity
and in his hand love, of ash wood
and loneliness,

walks towards us.

THE END JUSTIFIES

Disturbing a spider.
Swatting a mosquito.
Trampling a cricket.
Blowing up a frog.
Gouging out the eyes of a bird.
Flogging a horse to death.
Breaking an old woman's legs.
Letting a child drown.
Shooting ten people.
Murdering thousands of people, like rabid dogs.
Letting everybody, including myself, die in an instant.

But do I really need to save the world?

NO ONE CAN SERVE TWO MASTERS

Two masters
and the one master wants me to be afraid of death
and the other master wants me to ignore death altogether—

death is so insignificant!
It is so inescapable!
Shrug your shoulders!
Shudder!
Fall asleep!
Recoil!

Two masters
and I tell them I can't serve them both.

This makes them laugh,
merrily, heartily and scornfully.

And in the wings another is waiting—
sometimes I catch a glimpse of him.

ONE SWALLOW

You,
you were a swallow,
the first swallow,

and you made seven summers
without a single winter in between.

FROM THE ANSWER TO THE CORINTHIANS

... they are beautiful words.
We've looked at them from all angles.
We've even clothed them and let them dance.
They were hopeless at it.
They stepped on each other's toes, clutched each other
and fell over.
We had to help them up—they couldn't get up by themselves.
We sat them down in an easy chair.
They're asleep now.
They're snoring.
When they wake up we'll see what happens.
If they wake up, that is.

All that remains for us is unrest, longing and awkwardness,
those three,
and of those three, awkwardness the most.

LONG AGO

Long ago
I went for a walk and came to a wall.

Where was happiness? On this side.
Where was the truth? On this side.
Where did the sun shine? On this side.
Where was I free? On this side.

I kicked the wall.
I searched for a hole in the wall.

Then I took a few steps back,
closed my eyes, lowered my head,
took a deep breath.

MY FRIEND

My friend,
he's standing on the edge of a precipice,
but he doesn't falter,

those who claim he's faltering
don't know what faltering is,

it looks like faltering,
it even looks like falling,
like wanting to cling to something,
but it isn't,

it isn't shouting either
what he does,
or recoiling, or hesitating, or looking back,

it's something new,
something different,
something no one else can do—

my friend,
his blue sky,
his peregrine impatience,
his ash-grey, winter-perfect immortality,

he doesn't falter.

WHAT TWO WOMEN SAW

Two women saw someone drowning—
they just happened to be walking past,
happened to look in the direction of the person drowning—

they stopped, what should they do,
they looked at the arms flailing in the air,
listened to the cries for help
and brooded,
knitted their foreheads
and brooded as deeply as possible—

then they knew the answer:
we should be ashamed, they said,
nodding at each other—

it was a fine day, the sun was shining,
they stretched out in the grass under a willow
on the banks of the river
in which someone cried out one last time, surfaced one last time
and then drowned,
they hugged each other and felt ashamed,
deeply ashamed—
never did two women feel more ashamed
than those two women then.

NO

I wanted to say no,
I knew all about no, knew dozens of noes:
profound noes, half-hearted noes, faded noes, feisty noes—

I heard the sweet music of denial
and wanted to say a new no,
a clear no that would sparkle in the light of the setting sun,
an overwhelming no that would tower over the truth,
an infallible no,

but I said yes.

A LETTER

I have ice-cold fingers.
(But they don't tremble. Never!)

I write an icy letter,
a letter so cold that the air around it
freezes.
I keep getting up
    to breathe somewhere else.
Everything I write is true.

Halfway through the letter I suddenly write,
after a long, icy summing up:
'And yet…'

whereupon the letter defrosts
and floats off to sea,
unread.

YOU SHOULD

You should always be a little bit sad,
otherwise you're lost,

but you should be a little bit lost—
lost beyond hope—
otherwise you'd only be happy,

but you should be happy too,
able to be happy for no reason,
beside yourself with happiness,

otherwise you'd be sad,
a little bit sad
always.

A MOMENT

I found a moment,
it was just a moment,

but there they came already,
heavily armed
and in full regalia,
they came to guard it.

'That moment, over there!'

They were angry and in a hurry:
so many moments arising out of nothing,
while everything that's eternal perishes.

Still it remained unguarded,
it was a moment,
my moment.

TWO WOMEN

Two women.
There! Look! Those two specks!
They've reached such heights!
And still they're moving higher!
Or have they reached the highest point already
and are they falling?
Who can say?

It's summer.
The sun is shining.
There's a scent of raked hay, of pines, of wood fires,
of apple pie.

They've tossed each other so high up into the air...

It's late in the afternoon.
Will they remember to catch each other again
later,
or might they forget that
and get up, lost in thought,
dust off their clothes and leave,
oblivious of the thud, the cloud of dust behind them?

They eat cherries, they chase away mosquitoes, they see wagtails,
black redstarts.
It grows dark. They hear an owl. They wrap their arms
round each other.
Mustn't forget, they whisper. We mustn't forget.
There is something we mustn't forget.
No.

A MAN

A man existed,
he was sure he existed,

and not just any old way, he thought,
but utterly and significantly and acutely,

and he got knocked off his feet, chucked into ravines,
torn apart, shredded, trampled on,
blown away and set fire to,

but he went on existing,
went on and on existing—

how profoundly I exist… he thought,
how sure I am of *that*…!

and he thought of all those who aren't certain of that
and who don't exist
and who in all probability—if not absolutely certainly—
                                   have never existed
and never will exist,

and he shook his head, his big, far-reaching, all-embracing head
                                              over them.

MY FATHER APPLIED A DOUBLE STANDARD

My father
applied a double standard,
was Cain and Abel,
beat himself to death

my mother was already worm-eaten in those days
and my brothers were chickens born without heads

golden promises loomed on no horizon yet

my father cried:
'surely I am not my own keeper?'

'you are! you are!' the earth droned

my father buried himself,
the first dog eyed him with curiosity.

MY FATHER CREATED THE WORLD

My father
created the world:
heaven and earth,
simplicity and ambivalence,
gluttony and shabbiness,
my brothers and their rage,
but not my mother

'she's not finished yet,' he would say
whenever the sun came up
which he had earmarked for the sky
and allowed to shine through curtains

and there was fighting in the streets and in the squares,
bad judgement was rampant,
false promises were made,
and there was dying and squandering

peace had to wait
until my mother was finished—
she lacked will.

MY FATHER FISHED FOR ANSWERS

My father
fished for answers,
found none,
but he sang

real fishermen float in silence, crowned with glory,
with their bellies up, like chairmen of boards
drifting out to sea

my father sang about patient endurance
and about hunger that gnawed at him,
wanted something of him,
refused to tell him what it was

grinding his teeth while he sang softly

and my mother heard him
and took him with her—
didn't tell him where—
pushed him gently backwards on a bed,
nestled herself on top of him

and they became entangled
in the space that stretched beyond the furthest stars
                                   and induced the deepest sleep,
the great slovenly unknown.

MY FATHER SLEPT THROUGH HEADACHES

My father
slept through headaches, hazards and uncontrollable
                      feelings of inferiority,
slept through my mother,
slept through unrest and sorrow

my father established a wilderness of sleep
                      and inevitable fatigue,
slept my brothers to the end of his tether,
                      floating gently in the wind,
coldly and maliciously slept the light out of his face,
slept pity to death

my father slept with all summers, winters,
                      slept with the tide,
wrapped girls, dogs round him in his sleep

sparrows howled, swallows blared,
heaven and earth shook him, spat on him,
growled in his colossal, incredibly sharp ears

but my father slept
        like a thousand logs
in the moonlight
on the banks of a river.

MY FATHER WAS GONE

My father
was gone,
but not really

my mother and my brothers fumbled
               with their insecurity, unflagging,
muttered:
'he's gone forever'
but he wasn't really gone for ever,
'he's gone completely'
but he wasn't really gone completely,
'he's gone irrevocably'
but he wasn't really gone irrevocably

even the realest thing
        is not the very realest thing

darkness fell, thrushes sang in trees
              of dubious charm,
and everything uninhabited became even more uninhabited,
but my father,
my tiny, tiny, irrelevant father,
was not quite really, really gone.

MY FATHER EXPLAINED HIMSELF

My father
explained himself

my mother took leave of her senses
and my brothers sought refuge in relative things,
         matchsticks, yarn, washing-up liquid

it was a fine day
and my father tried
    with all the means at his disposal
       to love truly and genuinely,
           and love no less than everyone,
stood on his toes,
bit his nails,
held his breath…

but my mother and my brothers
               were open to only one explanation
and then no more,
and evening came
and my father whispered: 'reign of terror, reign of terror…'

MY FATHER BOWED TO THE INEVITABLE

My father
bowed to the inevitable
and my mother slept with him,
wept over the incomprehensible
    and the great all-embracing improbable

morning came
and my brothers saw her tears,
set fire to my father

and the inevitable rose from his ashes,
with dignity and mercy,
blowing kisses and casting meaningful glances,
while tripping over its own inevitability from time to time

and silence came
and unenlightenment—of a transparent kind—
and those who knew something nodded their heads

my mother slowly slept her way downstream
from upland plains.

MY FATHER WAS ALREADY HIMSELF

My father
was already himself,
my mother was still a young girl,
my brothers so very unborn
        that they sparkled in the sun

'are you coming…' my mother asked,
she was wearing red shoes
        and her mother's corals,
she had glitters on her nails
        and in her long red hair,
but dumbness struck my father,
chased him away

stalks snapped, frogs blew themselves up
and everything that shone evaporated

it was May
and my father didn't know that he would never be anyone
but himself
and that he lacked something,
something painful,
something invaluable of no consequence

and that summer was in the air,
and something misleading,
over and over again.

MY FATHER PROMISED EVERYTHING

My father
promised everything, pledged everything—
'even love?' my mother asked—
'everything'—
'even, even...' she searched for a word
that was greater than happiness—
'everything!' my father cried, 'or don't you know
what everything is?'
and he gave her everything
and my mother burnt down

then my father walked across seas and oceans,
his voice echoed by the earth's aversion,
the stiffness of the years

he was still thinking, he cried,
about dissolution and syrup!
'patience! patience!'

and he promised a golden spider in a golden web
and billions of golden flies of a devastating short-sightedness
in the radiant dawn of insanity

my father was so alone...

MY FATHER WANTED TO LOVE MY MOTHER

My father
wanted to love my mother,
wanted nothing more profoundly than that

and he gave her innocence and unpredictability
and fine promises
    that she had to live up to,
but it was not enough

then he gave her my brothers
and fistfuls of down-and-outs and charitableness
and—for lack of anything better—
melancholy and meaningful boredom,
but it was still never enough

my father didn't know what more he could do,
he wanted so badly to love her...

and he bent over her
and gave her rain
and inconsolability
and relentless nights

and he loved her.

MY FATHER GOT UNDER THE SKIN

My father
got under the skin
    of the placid,
invented subterfuge and self-deception,
destroyed consciences

my mother and my brothers wept
(they cursed, spat and shouted,
but they called it weeping)

and evening came
and my father collected giggling young girls
who caused little mishaps—
'oh sorry! sorry!' they sobbed
and tumbled into his arms—
and he made an end to assumptions
about his true nature

my father was a crow
who was nevertheless incorruptible,
perched on pitch-black branches
and croaked: 'corrupt me! corrupt me!'
and who was wizened
and without faith
and underexposed
and who fizzled out
one day.

MY FATHER WAS SO SMALL

My father
was so small,
so utterly senselessly irreparably small,
but no one asked him to become bigger and have more sense

my mother caressed him and clasped him in her arms,
my brothers asked themselves
whether they had ever wondered about him

my father,
inventor of miserliness and thoughtlessness,
rolled up his cosmic sleevelets

sparrows chirped in gutters and in hedges,
dew shimmered on wobbly cobwebs

and my father spat on the earth—tiny, lucid splodges—
and attacked heaven—little slaps, little kicks—
but no one asked him to call it a day
and become visible, divisible and considerable

my father, my paltry father,
my little Goliath.

MY FATHER WAS COMING TO AN END

My father
was coming to an end,
overflowed the banks of his will

my mother let him ripple, surge,
and my brothers set their course by him,
rocked on the long waves
               of his decline,
fished for the secrets
               he no longer possessed,
let him think,
let him be unable to put anything into words

evening came
and his sun let itself go under in him,
let him grow cold and remote,
his storms died down
and his winter beckoned to him: here! here!

but my father was asleep—
his gulls were tired
and settled on him.

MY FATHER BEGAN TO CONFUSE THINGS

My father
began to confuse things
      for want of people, thoughts

my mother embraced him,
took things out of his hands

then he was left with my brothers,
but they were growing twisted and entangled
till they became one single brother of no significance at all

then he opened himself
and elephants appeared, and white doves, ants, irises
      in the chinks of his mind,
but not for long,
my mother closed him again

and it turned cold
and my father was like a lamb
      for want of death.

MY FATHER WAS SOMETHING

My father
was something
no one could put their finger on

nice, said my mother,
but he wasn't nice,
brave, everything,
but he wasn't brave and not everything either

gone, said my brothers, unmistakable, inconceivable,
inconvenient...

they rubbed their hands:
'we'll get to the bottom of it,' they cried,
'don't worry!'...

sad, people said who didn't know him,
but he wasn't sad,
alone,
but he wasn't alone,
everybody,
nor everybody nor large nor shy
nor a crying shame

and the sun went down,
blackbirds were singing,
    but so beautifully and so naturally...
and spring came
and my father pointed at me.

MY MOTHER

My mother stood in the doorway,
she stood there in a blue dress with a red waistband,
her hair was tousled,
my brothers called out for her to come inside

my mother always did what they asked,
but she no longer knew what was inside
and what outside

she went outside,
this is inside, she thought, this must be inside,
everyone is here

it was a fine day
and everyone was there, everyone, everyone,
she took a deep breath
and didn't think of my father

I thought you were always thinking of him, she thought,
yes, but now I am not thinking of him

everyone loved her, that was obvious,
and loved her more and more, more wildly, more hungrily

how odd, my mother thought,
why do they do that,
she cast down her eyes

and my brothers called her again,
slammed their fists on the table,
plates bounced up, glasses toppled over

and my mother went inside
and thought of my father,
spring had come, and no mercy.

ZENO

There are no answers.

The sun is shining.
The wind is blowing.
A tortoise looks over his shoulder
and sees Achilles standing there,
waving at him
and calling out: 'Tortoise! Wait for me!'

We should be absolutely inconsolable.

I WAS YOUNG

I was young
I invented a girl a summer
and a river
she wasn't tall she wore a lilac dress
red shoes a red belt
I kept inventing more and more
shoelaces the height of her heels
her particular cheeks
the murmuring of the river a willow tree
the length of her hair a yellow bow
a dark-red necklace and the sun

I was young
I wanted to be completely honest
(poems must be honest or at most impetuous)
I'm writing a book about no I told her
everyone in my book says no
shakes his head denies rejects refuses and disapproves
I like no
I cleared my throat cast down my eyes
I want to ask you something I said

and she said yes
before I'd even asked her anything

I'm writing a book I said
you're young she said

I was young
I invented girls

MY BROTHER

My brother,
he's granite

I walk round him,
there have to be holes in him, cracks:
I look for the words in him
that describe his despair,
I know they exist,
I can't find them

he wants to go somewhere and tugs at me:
I must walk next to him,
I must walk behind him,
I must walk in front of him,
I must fly above him,
I must carry him on my shoulders
and all at the same time

meanwhile he even vanishes from my sight,
my brother,
my heavy brother

surprise is not his thing.

WINGS

I was still a child,
though not tiny any more,
I felt my shoulders:
there were no wings,
I kept checking,
but I didn't have wings,
not even the beginning of wings
      or anything resembling wings

why don't you fly, everyone asked
I don't have wings, I said

I didn't have wings,
I was a boy who lacked wings

and I took off and flew away,
in search of wings.

LOVE AND DEATH

However big death is,
there is always an even bigger death
that is indifferent

and however small love is,
there is always an even smaller love
that is untraceable,
like a grain of sand
at the bottom of the sea
in the Mariana Trench.

SORRY

I am sorry.

Those three words!
born out of disenchantment
    and a smattering of thoughtlessness

they matured in the dismal middle ground
between joy and pain

they marched through life
one two one two,
dreaming of being seen

and they changed their meaning imperceptibly,
turned pale
in the sight of unseeing strangers

divine and in vain

oh, I'm sorry, I'm sorry!

TO ERR

Is erring human,
isn't it divine?

And shame,
shouldn't that be the only truly divine emotion—
heavenly shame,
the reason why the divine makes itself small,
conceals itself
and pulls its immortal grey hairs out of its
       grey immanence, in the dark,
while we bow our heads and whisper
that we forgive,
that we don't blame it in any way—
we wouldn't dare—
and that we too err from time to time?

But we don't err.
Not like that.

DISTANCE

The distance between dead and almost dead
is improbably small

and those who double-check that distance and record it
and compare their measurements with earlier ones,
find their hair standing on end in amazement

in the evening they sit at table,
chatting about the events of their day
with those who stubbornly claim
that they love them and will never
abandon them

it's autumn,
the distance between living and almost living
immeasurably great.

DAUGHTER

She pushes barbed wire aside,
her fingers are bleeding,
she looks pale, she's cold

beyond the barbed wire are shrubs,
still bare and thorny,
'Walk round them!' voices press her

she walks through them
and roses begin to blossom, spread their scent,
timid roses everywhere

beyond the shrubs the sun is shining, she sits down there,
there's moss and there are butterflies,
peacock butterflies, emperor moths, pintails, foxes

she leans back, she's my daughter,
she doesn't look back,
she doesn't want to turn into anything else.

TOO FAR INTO THE SEA

People swim too far into the sea,
raise their arms in the air,
but they can't think of the word 'help'

they call out other words,
words that tumble across each other,
whole sentences, treatises, credos,
they can think of everything,
but not of that word, that one word

rescuers stand on the beach and wait—
they're patient, but not endlessly,
they're hungry,
they've got families to think of

and those swimmers keep calling out,
their arms flailing,
their words ever wilder, shriller and more profound

A POEM FOR HENRY HUDSON

My father
lay in the arms of my mother,
my brothers entered the room, asked:
'Are we in your way?'
pulled him to his feet,
gave him a good shaking, shouted:
'We want to know now! Are we in your way?!'—
but my father tore himself loose
and vanished inside my mother—
philosophers rushed forward, searched for him in vain,
fumbled at the gates of life,
pulled answers out of their hats in desperation

and water fell on the barren heath and between the wild corn,
sparkled in the sun, enticing butterflies, wolves,
carved a path through pine forest and birches,
quenched the thirst of Indians, bears and deer,
wondered at the immense silence
              of the world all around,
carried death and life and uncertainty along with it,
stumbled into chasms,
seethed with rage and pulled itself together again,
wrestled its way through cracks and crevices,
called out to the tiniest and most timid of brooks:
'I am a river. Come with me!'
'Whereto?'
'To the sea!'
'To the sea?'
'Yes, to the sea!'
saw the sea
and sighed the way only a river can sigh
out of immortality and melancholy,
nestled in the arms of a bay and slept,
until one day—ships sailed by
and the river awoke, opened its mouth wide,
cried: 'Hudson! You! I have been waiting for you! I knew you

would come!'
and Henry Hudson put his telescope to one eye
              and called out to his sailors:
'This is where we are meant to be!
This is the centre of the world.'

I went to the centre of the world,
I wanted to hear Thelonious Monk,
John Coltrane at the Village Vanguard
              playing the first notes of 'My favourite things',
I wanted to go to Minton's Playhouse on a Monday night
and hear Charlie Parker play 'I got rhythm', each time in a
    different key,
I wanted to see the Yankees, witness Casey Stengel come out
    of the dugout,
hear the Moose call for Moose Skowron,
see Mickey Mantle hit a first pitch into the bleachers—
I would never bet against them—
I wanted to see Roosevelt Grier, Sam Huff, Dick Modzelewski,
    Jim Katcavage and Andy Robustelli
standing unshakeable on the goal line in Yankee Stadium,
the Rocky Mountains of my imagination,
I wanted to take the ferry to Staten Island for a nickel
and eat one of Nathan's footlong hotdogs on Coney Island,
with chilli, pickles and extra mustard,
I wanted to see the Ferris wheel and walk along the boardwalk,
like the father and mother of Delmore Schwartz in an
    irresponsible dream once,
I wanted to be a poet, make girls gaze at me in wonder,
run their hands through my hair,
wake up beside one of them, one morning, for the first time,
I wanted to walk where Jimmy Walker had walked,
              at the head of the Police Parade,
I wanted to let him know, my Jimmy, my hero,
that I would still love him in December,
even if it meant trudging through the snow,
I wanted to hear LaGuardia—Oh Fiorello, how I love you too!—
as he read the daily cartoons on the radio,
I wanted to think:

here Joe Louis, the 'great brown bomber', would saunter
 between two fights,
and here walked Ray Robinson in his sugar-pink coat, a girl on
 each arm,
I wanted to nod at Jack Dempsey through the window of his
 restaurant
and slowly, very slowly, count to ten, without him noticing,
I wanted to sound a barbaric yawp over the roofs of Brooklyn,
 like Walt Whitman,
I wanted to close my eyes tight and cheer Lafayette in Fulton Street
and the GI's along Broadway in '45,
I wanted to be at the centre of the world,
which was once in Voorstraat, on the corner of Asylstraat,
in a small town in Holland,
but had now changed places and was here—
I was just a boy, still wearing the wrong clothes,
blushing each time someone asked me a question—
I wanted to see subways ride past, 'whole cars', 'whole trains'
by Dondi, Lee, Rammellzee and Blade,
I wanted to know where e.e. cummings gave his capitals to the
 garbage man,
where Dutch Schultz drew his final breath with his head in his plate
and where on 15 June 1904—the day before Bloomsday—
the General Slocum went down with more than a thousand
 children on board,
the greatest disaster in the ninety-seven years that followed,
I wanted to be here, stay here, far away
and yet nowhere so close

and morning came,
philosophers slept their hermetic sleep,
the sun rose
and my father crawled out of my mother,
became immense, grey and almighty,
stretched out his arms—
my brothers, my millions of brothers,
swarming at his feet—
and he said:

'No, you are not in my way.
You are never in my way,'

and my mother wept.

SUNSET

The sun is going down.
I'm sitting on a rock in the middle of the desert.
My desert.
It is my sun that is setting, behind my horizon.
I think of everything I have been and still am today:
unworkable, unsound, unthinking, unfathomed, unripened,
un… how shall I put it?
Why am I not simply unhappy?
But to this day—for some obscure reason—
I am still not that.

IT WAS RAINING

It was raining
and the air was full of suspicion and despondency

and an angel appeared,
looked around
and struck someone down,
and then another person,
and another person

and at the rear, in the dark, behind everyone,
cowering, with his back against a wall,
a man was sitting, looked at the ground
and thought,
thought for days months years
and finally, one morning,
in a fit of recklessness—gulls
screeching in the pale air—thought:
I, I will…

and the angel worked his way towards him.

I'VE COME TO FIGHT WITH YOU

I've come to fight with you, said an angel—
a man was silent—
I will keep haunting you,
I will strike you until you bleed, drag you after me
and never let go of you…

the angel blew a bit of fluff off one of his giant wings

…I love you

the man said nothing.

A MAN THOUGHT THAT HE WAS FREE

A man thought that he was free
and an angel struck him down

the man said that he was free
and again the angel struck him down

the man said once again that he was free
and once again the angel struck him down

then the man shouted that he was free,
that he was always free, that he would never be anything but free,
but the angel struck him until he bled

and shame and wasted effort blew about
and spread like dust
across the grey earth

and the man stammered that he was free,
that he thought that he was free

and the angel flew away.

AN ANGEL LOOKED AT A MAN

An angel looked at a man,
but the man said: I am looking at myself

the angel fought with the man,
but the man said: I am fighting with myself

the angel beat the man almost to death,
but the man said: I am beating myself almost to death

the angel bent over the man
and comforted him,
but the man cried: I am bending over myself,
I am comforting myself!

then the angel flew away
and the man got up, threw stones after him,
shouted:
as if I can fly…!

fell out of the blue, brightly lit sky.

A MAN SAID: I CAN'T LIVE

A man said:
I can't live,
and he lived long and meticulously

then he stood still and said:
I can't love,
and he loved women and peace
              and unspoken shyness

and an angel descended, fought with him—
I can't fight, said the man
and he fought like a tiger, like a hare
              and like a bag of bones

the sun went down and still they fought on,
the man and the angel,
and the man said:
now I know, I can't lose.

A WARM DAY

It was a warm day,
I can't go on, a man thought,
an angel was fighting with him
and said: neither can I

evening came,
one of us must beg for mercy,
the angel gasped,
yes, gasped the man, one of us

the moon came up
and the world was large and pale,
surged around them,
they wiped the blood off their faces
and slowly continued their fight

one of us, the angel whispered,
yes, the man whispered, one of us.

EVENING

Evening came,
are we done with fighting, a man asked,
we are done with fighting, an angel answered

and he lifted the man up, held him against the light
and said: you are transparent, now

you can let me go, said the man
and the angel nodded and let him go

the man blew away

and those left behind spoke about something they held in
higher esteem
than love, something black,
they didn't know what to call it, something bitter

or were they talking about death,
about a pig rooting around under a dead tree

or about the sea?

A MAN DECLARED WAR ON HIMSELF

A man declared war on himself,
marched against himself,
saw himself as an enormous army on the horizon,
equipped with the deadliest weapons,
saw himself prepare for a decisive battle,
dug himself in and waited

and an angel descended and gave the man a sign,
and one night he launched a massive surprise attack on himself,
and defeated himself after hours of savage battle

hoisted a flag on his unknown mangled self
in the first light of the morning sun

and went home to live in peace.

A MAN COLLECTED QUESTIONS

A man collected questions, uncertainties,
vague inklings, dubious assumptions,
wrong-headed conclusions, debatable motives,
misplaced convictions, mood swings,
painful states of mind, feverish fluctuations in character
and unremitting, conflicting thoughts about death

collected himself into the ground

and an angel touched him very gently, very carefully
                and with the greatest possible tenderness
and autumn came
and the wind lifted the man up and blew him away

children, a few small children, caught a last glimpse of him dancing
on the rays
of the setting sun.

A MAN IS FIGHTING WITH AN ANGEL

A man is fighting with an angel—

and one day death will enter,
in his infinite charitableness he will take off his jacket
and close the door after him

he will sit down,
having all the time in the world

he will solve an equation with dozens of unknowns
and disclose one secret (just one)

then he will be silent
and simply point to the dust which, like a girl,
dances in the sunlight between the curtains—

fight with an angel, fight.

IN THE END

In the end,
if we just wait long enough,
if we have seen beauty change shape,
if we have seen justice bend over backwards,
if we realise that we have believed in something impossible,
if we have cherished hope to the point of madness,
if we have loved until we grew withered and worm-eaten
and could not go on—
so help us what is left of our self-knowledge—
in the end,
out of everything that was
and could have been and should have been
in every fraction of our seconds,
there only remains
an I fighting with an angel,
night falls
and the angel strikes him down.

WINTER

It was winter
and an angel fought with a man,
struck him down, dragged him after himself,
flung him into a ravine,
flew away,
cried out, without looking back:
or shall we start all over again—
it's up to you

and the man thought about the sadness that he suspected
he felt then
and about the sun that was setting so slowly,
so agonisingly slowly,
and he whispered:
all right.

2010—The Present

THEY WHO CLIMB WITHOUT FALLING

They who climb without falling,
they reach the highest peaks,
they see the greatest and most glorious vistas,
they dance a few steps
    with an elegance and ease bordering on perfection
and bow to a huge audience
    in the dizzying depths beneath them

they know no fear, no premonition of pain and endless regret

they are wrong.

PAIN

Nothing is more ordinary than pain

nearly everything is ordinary,
waking up is ordinary,
getting up, the sun, a thrush,
the scent of resin, a twig that cracks under your foot,
the blue of the sky

intentions are ordinary, doubts, promises,
some promises—even solemn ones—
are in no way extraordinary at all

breaking your promises is also ordinary,
even more so than the promises themselves

but pain is the most ordinary
of all.

THE WRITER EXAMINES HIS WORDS

The writer examines his words—
what shall I write today... he wonders

he pulls out remorse, airs it
and puts it away again,
lets nevertheless run through his fingers,
inhales the scent of foolery,
muses over his worn-out sins on the ground

before choosing impatience and astuteness,
then he sits down at his table,
dressed in his customary I and me,
with his loyal hubris at his feet.

ALONE WITH THE READER

The writer wants to be alone with the reader

he wants the reader to be wise and receptive
    and to be on his way somewhere, with thousands, millions
    of others,
he wants him to hear the writer groan,
so that he stops and wonders where that almost inaudible
    sound is coming from,
    a sound barely attributable to a human voice,
he wants him to continue on his way with a vague sense of disquiet,
    perhaps even with a sense of guilt that has woken from its sleep,
he wants him to move on even more mindfully, placing his feet
    on him, whom he doesn't know,

and who is alone with him.

HOMECOMING

The writer comes home—
he's spent years brooding—
knocks on the door,
hears voices inside

I hope, he thinks, that my father will be there,
as I've got so much to tell him...

but his father is dead
and the reader opens the door
and immediately slams it in his face

the writer stands there,
pushes up his collar
and starts writing

he's lost, at last, now.

WORDS HE CAN'T WRITE

The writer comes up with words
that he can't write—
they're too slight, they dissolve, they keep scattering

the writer adds emphasis and engagement to make them weightier,
ties them to ancient words,
gives them animation

and the words begin to tear,
emitting a strange odour,
they can't handle their meaning

the writer tries to forget them,
but the words don't forget him,
cling to him,
lead him into temptation

where the reader waits for him.

THE WRITER CHERISHES

The writer cherishes beauty,
old hurts
and all the dissatisfaction in the world

his senses are strewn about like underwear, newspapers,
                          copies of *Ideal Home*

occasionally, when he's writing, his mother stands behind him,
shaking her head at him,
telling him not to hunch his shoulders but to hold his head
    up high

all that's left of her is her worry

she takes his pen from his hand and opens his window
and the writer remembers the beauty of grace
               and of not writing, not thinking and not being,
he hums like a bumblebee and disappears between the net curtains
into the great, blue nothingness.

THE DIFFERENCES

'Spot the differences! spot the differences!' the difference-
   monger cries
                    in the wild, unbridled evening light
and people look for the differences between their will and their desire,
scraping across the bedrock of their souls.

IN THE BEGINNING

In the beginning there was light
and God was blinded,
so he created people to extinguish it,
crying:
'Out! Out!'

even now he's afraid to open his eyes,
he's hoarse from shouting
and whispers: 'Out, out…'
even now light slips under doors, through cracks in walls,
between roof tiles, undergrowth

and even now there are people who don't want
his will to be done

they sail in little paper boats,
beaming at each other.

TRUST

I wish I could trust myself,
that I could rely on myself,
share my secrets with myself—
I certainly have them,
     but I don't know them

I know I'd like to shake myself awake
and tell myself everything I don't know

but I don't trust myself,
I let myself sleep

it's cold,
I cover myself with an extra blanket

I'm still in the dark.

REALITY

I wish reality was an object,
that I could touch it, pick it up and chuck it away

and that I'd find it again, whenever it suited me,
and I'd polish it
until it sparkled like a river in the sun

I wish truth was a mistake
and that everyone understood this and apologised for it

inside me lives an ant, larger than an elephant,
lazier than a lion

I wish there was something else, the beginning of something else.

THE IMPOSSIBLE

I wanted to make the impossible possible

I loved the impossible, loved nothing more passionately,
but I still wanted to make it possible,
with well-defined limits, straight angles, clear hues
and certainty, the certainty of I can and I will

but years later, when I wanted to make the possible impossible,
someone cried that I should hurry up and come inside,
why was I dilly-dallying like that,
there was still so much to do.

THE THOUGHT

A thought keeps stalking me, hounding me,
I can hear it, I can feel it breathing down my neck

but whatever it does, it won't get me,
with its gleaming fangs
    and its hunger and lust

I don't think it.

I WONDER

I know a man
                who is an abyss

roses grow along his walls
and the odd nervous little tree of the rarest breed

there are caverns in him,
with bats shooting out
in the evenings, when it grows dark

those who lean forward too far
tumble into him
and their fate can only be guessed at

there are huge warning signs on the roads that lead to him

there are patrols,
proposals for closing him, filling him in

I throw a pebble into him,
wondering whether I'll hear it land.

A GARDEN

I wish I was a garden
and that no one ever mowed my lawn,
picked flowers in me,
weeded me,
pruned my shrubs,
raked my paths,
dredged my ponds,
eradicated my lice,
and that nobody ever spaded me, levelled me up, covered me,
dug me out, fenced me in,
partitioned me, tiled me,
had me redesigned
by a highly-recommended landscape gardener,
                              praised to the skies in
Home and Garden,
or sold me

I wish somebody neglected me.

WEATHER FORECAST

Tomorrow we will see unsettled and unusual weather.
Instead of the sun rising at 05.24, a dog will rise,
a fiery red dog that will climb up through the sky,
wearing an iron chain round his neck,
and he will growl at the clouds
as they hastily make room for him.
At 13.37 he will be at the zenith and bark,
he'll bend forward and chase everyone inside
                        with his furious scowl.
'The dog is shining! The dog is shining!' everyone will whisper,
but the dog won't shine, the dog will yank at his chain
and bare his teeth.
Late in the afternoon he will descend to the horizon and howl.
Everyone will emerge again,
sit down on their benches outside their houses and cry:
'Oh dog, why are you howling…'
People will want to pat him and console him
or give him something to eat.
But no one will be able to reach him
and everyone will close their eyes and let the howling
wash over them.
At 21.51 the dog will set and never return.
The day after tomorrow the sun will shine again,
that big, round, dazzling thing that everyone's familiar with,
the most ordinary thing in the whole cosmos,
that had already existed for billions of years
before there was any mention
of a sky or a firmament,
and that does nothing but emerge from behind clouds,
rise, set and shine.
It will be a pleasant day.
But should you wonder, the day after tomorrow, why you're so sad,
it will be because you miss the dog,
the dog that will appear in the sky tomorrow.

FOR AN OLD FRIEND

I had a friend who was dying,
I watched him die,
I heard him die

I stood there
and with the greatest stretch of my empathy,
             which had so far proved useless,

I changed places with him

the difference was smaller than I'd expected

he watched me die,
heard me die

he stood there
and said that it was better this way, fairer,
how should he put it,
he still had so much to do, so much of consequence

he thanked me for my empathy
and for the incredible effectiveness
of its timing

it happened one morning in a forest,
he'd gone for a jog,
I died there.

WHAT TO SAY

I saw someone ponder,
I saw him ponder about me
       and what he would say after my death:
'he was my friend,'
but I wasn't his friend—
I saw the wrinkles in his brow,
       the drops of sweat in between,
how he felt responsible for the essence of his sadness

he was desperate,
I saw that he was desperate,
wishing with all his might that I would live a long life
or if not, that he would wake up one night,
knowing what I really was to him
and knowing what one can and cannot say about a dead person,
what is true and genuine
       and what is worth stretching the truth for,
and otherwise he'd say:
'I, I…'
and be unable to speak
and look for the handkerchief he'd deliberately forgotten

I wanted to be his friend,
his best friend,
       his pouring rain, his lack of sense.

A STRANGER

I wish I was complicated,
that I kept mystifying myself

a stranger who enters,
wearing my clothes, biting my nails

who tells me what to write,
quickly! before you've recovered from the shock!

who doesn't read what I've written—
he has enough on his mind
              that I know nothing about

who never tells me when he'll return
and least of all where he is
              when he's not here

who wishes he were me,
whiling away the time.

PONTIUS PILATE

When I look in the mirror
                    I see Pontius Pilate,
the curls around my ears, the pallor of my cheeks,
my aversion

I don't want this face,
I want a different face, that of Barabbas, or Jesus
or one of the two petty thieves
or someone from that crowd, if need be a woman in tears

contempt! *that's* the word I've been looking for all day,
to use in a letter that I *must* write

look at me! there will soon be news from Rome,
you'll be transferred
to god knows where.

PORTRAIT

I saw a man who was gentle
and who treasured gentleness
      the way a hunter treasures his rifle

I warned him:
gentleness is hazardous,
it procrastinates, hangs fire, undermines, spoils, debilitates...
without gentleness life is so much more pleasurable,
                      more acceptable too...

I saw him leave,
he had tears in his eyes, touched heaven with one hand
and agreed with me,
he always agreed with me

I stayed on my side of life,
I lacked the right kind of aversion to the here and now.

FRANCIS OF ASSISI

I saw Francis of Assisi run
                          along the borders of hysteria,
chased by dogs and wolves and Tsars with their boyars
                          and jaundice, scarlet fever, diphtheria

the sun went down and I saw a field mouse
                          trying to slip away quietly
through the grass at my feet

I was alone,
I had to choose between the known and the unknown

it was November,
the rain began to beat down violently
and someone called out:
'hey, you, lagging behind, get a move on,
or you'll die, cold and empty-handed!'

THERE'S SOMETHING IN THE AIR

There's something in the air,
some people claim it's Death,
they should know,
the vague contours... the lack of weight...

others say it's something else,
they too should know,
they are familiar with Death, have spoken with him, shaken his hand

a few have slept with him,
he was clumsy, they say, but tender, he took his time,
they don't know if it's him who's in the air,
they're scared to look

the odd one out grabs a ladder.

EVENING

Some people
refuse to face Death

they jump onto motor-bikes
and ride along the byways of self-respect
to dodge death

the death of bad habits
              and unfinished business

it's raining
and I wish I was a fish
and that there was no land any more,
no sand, no sun, no reeds,
no wisdom with hindsight,
no reality beyond reality,
no omens of any kind

just water and lack of evidence.

THE REARGUARD

In the rearguard the last uncorrupted ones
fan the fire of their imagination

and the fire crackles, spits out children
and fiery arguments

all is silent in the vanguard,
the Buddha carefully spreads out
      a neatly folded napkin,
attaches it to his shirt
and starts eating

in the rearguard the flames flare up higher and higher,
while the uncorrupted ones keep fanning
      the blaze of their imagination

and deliver terrible tidings.

HUNGER, PAIN AND ANGER

Hunger, pain and anger are drops in the ocean,
hatred is a smouldering coal,
war is a licence,
peace a coincidence,
longing a roadblock,
passion a closed book,
hubris a nervous condition,
jealousy a spanner in the works,
fear a makeshift solution,
shame a necessary evil,
guilt a bottomless pit,
sadness an incidental circumstance,
death an error of judgement,
love a lot of cooing,
I…
but that I is still waiting for an adequate comparison.

LOVING

There's something absurd about loving,
otherwise it wouldn't be loving—
dying is absurd too,
most definitely—
perhaps there's nothing more absurd than dying

in the morning I don't think of anything in particular,
in the afternoon I don't think,
in the evening I think of myself,
but at night I think of dying and of how it's somehow absurd,
I can prove it, it's very simple, really surprisingly simple,
there are a few loose ends still, loose ends not worth mentioning…

I certainly know there's something absurd about loving,
but I'll never be able to prove it.

THE FACE OF THE PAST

Snails are crawling across the face of the past,
a rose is blossoming in one eye:
it looks as if it's dead…
if only!

the past loves snails, loves loose sand on its cheeks,
loves roses in its eyes, worms in its ears

it doesn't move, but it's not asleep,
it keeps watch—
only the present is asleep—
the past whispers: 'Ssh…'

THE ENEMY

The enemy has won, our enemy,
but he doesn't know it yet

he wants the worst for us,
but he doesn't know that yet either

he lies on the ground, looks around, crestfallen

and see, there is the lamb,
the meek, bloodthirsty, impudent lamb,
it nestles against him, licks him, soothes him

and the enemy stands up,
for he knows now that he has won, he is among us.

MY MOTHER

Torn lace curtains, torn responsibilities—
they've felled my mother,
she sits up:
'are you one of them?'

but I was busy avoiding, escaping, absenting myself
                               among jackals and lions

I wish I was stronger
and could carry her suffering on my shoulders—
why does my mother still bother with me?

it's winter, she's at the window, between the lace curtains,
I face her—between us glass and shame—
my mother.

SHE WHO SHAKES HER HEAD

She who shakes her head,
who doesn't let anything escape her attention and shakes her head,
who broods and considers and reconsiders and shakes her head,
who intends and changes her mind and shakes her head,
who is at an utter loss, bites her tongue and shakes her head,
who loves someone deeply and still shakes her head,
                                  cannot but shake her head

who is dead and looks down and still shakes
                                        her dear dear head.

THE FACE OF SIMPLICITY

The face of simplicity has been torn up.
Someone wanted to throw it away: what's the use of simplicity?
Pigeons on the edge of my balcony.
The simplicity of searching for food and not thinking of
    Death, who is present every day... every minute...
My brother is dead.
His face looks at me, its two torn halves.
Can anyone repair simplicity?
'*Simplicity Repairs*: we repair anything that has
    lost its simplicity.'
I enter with the face of my brother.
'Can you repair this?'
'Let's see. Yes, that should be fine. Come back in a week's time.'
But when I come back after a week—I've kept the receipt,
    I don't want to be given the wrong face:
'I'm sorry, it fell apart in my hands. Was the person
    whose face it was truly simple? Are you sure?'
I look down at the floor.
'I suspect he wasn't, but I do have something else for you,
    to make up for the loss. I can see you're inconsolable.'
I put it on and look around.
Everything is new, but I miss my brother.

THEY OVERLOOK ONE

They kill people, bend over them
and kill them again

'they're already dead,' I say,
'they can't be dead enough,' they reply

they seal the dead down
and, to be absolutely sure, kill them again and then again,
so that I'll never be able to think of them any more

but they overlook one.

WHO'S THERE?

Me! It's me!
I'm sailing towards heaven on a phantom ship,
I've had a lucky escape—if only I knew what I've escaped

I've eaten all the phantoms,
I was starving,
they danced on my tongue...

now I'm sailing towards the stars,
like a sated showman
        resting under the mountain ash of happiness,
and with the speed of a snail with crystal eyes,
grunting like a piglet
        while God beats his drum for him

hillbillies we are, tossed about, like coyotes in the storm,
until our grunts become whispers
and nobody hears us any more,
        nobody hears us any more...

MY NEIGHBOUR

They hold his face right up to mine,
this is him! your neighbour! love him!

I see how wretched and racked he is,
I wish I didn't care about him

he shakes his head, he's almost dead...
don't do it, he says, don't love me, don't do it...

he wrings himself loose
and everything starts spinning, whirling,
everything is so childishly simple.

Unpublished Poems

A WOMAN

I knew a woman who wanted to be happy
and this woman rose and this woman went down,
unclouded one moment and overcast the next,
thundering, flashing and freezing
                almost to death,
this woman went icy and hailed and snowed,
she fluttered down from the sky and rained,
misted up windows, pattered on roofs, dripped from hair,
drifted past and shone,
                sparkled

sometimes she would suddenly erupt,
quickly swelling to a hurricane,
blowing everything and everyone along with her
or sending things flying,
before dying down unexpectedly again—
                so not a blade of grass moved

at other times she hung close to the ground, ever closer and denser,
limiting the view to centimetres, millimetres,
making foghorns blare
before lifting again at great speed,
                to become a ray of sunshine

Mrs. Unforecastable, they called her,
affectionately

she wanted to be happy,
simply happy

ON DEATH

I don't want to talk about death any more—
I start every encounter, every conversation by saying:
'let's not talk about death'

if someone says:
'nice weather today'
I say:
'certainly not weather for discussing death'

I tell everyone that death is such a mundane,
                            not to say banal topic—
you'd think there's nothing else to talk about:
love, for instance…
but no, death, death, always death…
I refuse to answer any more questions about it,
or fill in questionnaires,
or take part in conferences and chat shows on the subject

if someone asks:
'are you coming to the beach with us?'
I say:
'only if we don't mention death even once all day'

and then I go to the beach,
but alone—
the other person can't possibly live up to my demand—
I dig a hole in silence
and from that hole I watch the surf, the sun, a freighter,
a yacht, gulls, children, kites, surfers,
dogs running about freely, dark clouds appearing on the horizon,
I toss back a ball that comes rolling my way,
I put a towel over my head,
rub sun lotion on my nose and cheeks
and with almost superhuman willpower
that fills me with immense pride,
I stop thinking about death.

A CUPBOARD

I wish I was a cupboard that couldn't open any more,
and that I was a boy who was standing in front of me,
fumbling at my door,
laying my ear against me
thinking I overheard something, something shocking,
                    something of vital importance

I wish I was standing in a corner of a room like this,
even though I was empty,
with woodworms drilling holes in me

after all we all decay,
such a cupboard I imagined

I wish I was a boy.

HAPPINESS

I wish I knew whether I was happy

if I knew it, I'd stop dead in my tracks,
for what would be the point of continuing?

they who are unhappy would see me
and point at me:
'look, over there, someone who's happy!'

they'd run past me in a hurry,
to a place where I'm no longer welcome

if I was happy, I'd be inconsolable.

ON DESPAIR

I don't want to despair,
no matter what happens,
no matter what pain, adversity or inexplicable inner chaos
strikes me

I get anxious
when I detect even a hint of despair in myself
and with steely patience I pull myself together

at night I lie awake, keep myself awake,
scared that I'll wake up in despair one morning,
for no reason at all

I know my despair will be irrevocable then,
irredeemable as death

I'm made of glass, I think, I mustn't shatter

look, people say, when they see me walk by,
that man there, that cheerful man, he's just a few steps short
                                                of despair.

MY FEELINGS

I wish I could express my feelings

sometimes I hook them out at night:

Oh feelings,
dear little feelings,
why can I never find words for you,
you're so beautiful, so sweet...

then they bite me, jeer at me,
beautiful? sweet? we're not beautiful and sweet at all!
be glad!

my god, how they despise me...

then I fall asleep,
with lockjaw, a sardonic grin,
                      the hullabaloo of a breath of wind.

A STRAW

I wish there was a field full of straws,
thousands of straws, waving gently in the wind

summer went by and one by one they snapped,
shrivelled up—
there was just one left,
'you may as well take that one,' someone said

I took that straw, the last one, clutching it tightly—
it didn't snap or shrivel up

and I never let go of it again.

THE PRECIPICE

I'm standing before a precipice—
my precipice
that is one millimetre deep and one millimetre wide

my contempt for death dawdles.

DUTCH SOURCE TEXTS:

Pp. 11–12: *De zin van een liguster*, Querido, Amsterdam 1980

Pp. 13–18: *De Aanzet tot een web*, Querido, Amsterdam 1981

Pp. 19–21: *Beroemde scherven*, Querido, Amsterdam 1982

Pp. 22–33: *De andere ridders*, Querido, Amsterdam 1984

Pp. 34–41: *Mijn winter*, Querido, Amsterdam 1987

Pp. 42–43: *In N. en andere gedichten*, Querido, Amsterdam 1989

Pp. 44–53: *Een langzame val*, Querido, Amsterdam 1991

Pp. 54–60: *Een dansschool*, Querido, Amsterdam 1992

Pp. 61–65: *Tijger onder de slakken*, Querido, Amsterdam 1994

Pp. 66–81: *Als we vlammen waren*, Querido, Amsterdam 1996

Pp. 82–94: *Over liefde en over niets anders*, Querido, Amsterdam 1997

Pp. 95–108: *Gewone gedichten*, Querido, Amsterdam 1998

P. 109: *Gedichten 1977–1999*, Querido, Amsterdam 2000

Pp. 113–114: *Kruis en munt*, Querido, Amsterdam 2000

Pp. 115–123: *De een en de ander*, Querido, Amsterdam 2001

P. 124: *Lof der zotheid*, Amsterdam, Querido, Amsterdam 2001

Pp. 125–128: *Ik wou*, Lannoo, Tielt 2001

Pp. 129–131: *Alleen liefde*, Querido, Amsterdam 2002

Pp. 132–134: *Wie A Zegt*, Querido, Amsterdam 2004

Pp. 135–137: *Minuscule oorlogen*, Querido, Amsterdam 2004

Pp. 138–142: *Daar zijn woorden voor*, Muntinga, Amsterdam 2005

Pp. 143–144: *Wachten op wonderen*, Stichting CBK Zeeland, Middelburg 2005

Pp. 145–160: *Raafvogels*, Querido, Amsterdam 2006

Pp. 161–170: *Hemels en vergeefs*, Querido, Amsterdam 2008

Pp. 171–174: *Een gedicht voor Henry Hudson* (Poetry International Web)

P. 175: *Het vertrek van de mier*, Querido, Amsterdam 2009

Pp. 176–187: *Stof dat als een meisje*, Querido, Amsterdam 2009

Pp. 191–192: *Het wezen van de olifant*, Querido, Amsterdam 2010

Pp. 193–197: *Schrijver en lezer,* Querido, Amsterdam 2011
P. 198: *De verschillen,* Philip Elchers, Groningen 2013
Pp. 199–212: *De werkelijkheid,* Querido, Amsterdam 2014
Pp. 213–225: *Glas tussen ons,* Querido, Amsterdam 2018

ENGLISH COLLECTIONS FROM WHICH SOME OF THE TRANSLATIONS WERE TAKEN:

Pp. 82–94: *About Love and About Nothing Else,* Shoestring Press, Nottingham 2008

Pp. 171–174: *A Poetic Celebration of the Hudson River,* Carcanet Press, Manchester 2009

Pp. 145–160: *Raptors,* Carcanet Press, Manchester 2011

Pp. 176–187: *A Man and an Angel,* Shoestring Press, Nottingham 2013

ABOUT THE AUTHOR

Toon Tellegen was born in 1941 on one of the islands in the south-west of the Netherlands. He is one of Holland's most celebrated poets, with many awards to his name. In 2007 he was given two major prizes for his entire oeuvre. He considers himself in the first place a poet and has written more than twenty collections to date, but he is also a novelist and extremely popular children's book author. Tellegen lives in Amsterdam with his wife, and worked as a GP until his retirement. He frequently gives readings of his work, often to musical accompaniment. His work has been translated into many languages. His collection *Raptors*, translated by Judith Wilkinson, was published by Carcanet in 2011 and awarded the Popescu Prize. One of his children's books, *Letters to Anyone and Everyone,* published by Boxer Books in 2010, won the Marsh Award for Children's Literature in Translation.

ABOUT THE TRANSLATOR

Judith Wilkinson is a British poet and translator living in the Netherlands. She has won many awards, including the Popescu Prize for European poetry in translation (for Tellegen's *Raptors*) and the Brockway Prize. Her other translations of work by Tellegen are *About Love and about Nothing Else* (Shoestring, 2008), *Raptors* (Carcanet, 2011) and *A Man and an Angel* (Shoestring, 2013). She has also translated books by, among others, Miriam Van hee (a PBS Recommendation), Hagar Peeters and Menno Wigman (forthcoming). Two collections of her own work have been published by Shoestring.